SUPERMEN II

**THE 2003
PATRIOTS
AND THEIR
SECOND
SUPER
SEASON**

TRIUMPH
BOOKS

In the depths of Reliant Stadium in Houston, in the hours before Super Bowl XXXVIII, coach Bill Belichick told his team the simple truth: "We're the champions and the trophy is coming back where it belongs."

The New England Patriots of 2003-04 did indeed bring the Vince Lombardi Trophy back home with a thrilling 32-29 victory over Carolina in the Super Bowl. But that is only part of the story. Along the way, the team won 15 in a row (second best in NFL history) and did whatever needed to be done.

"I've never been a part of such a gritty team," running back Antowain Smith would say later. "Whatever we went up against, we always found a way to win the game. We've got a bunch of players that believe in each other. Fifteen wins in a row, that's something that I never imagined I'd be a part of. It was hard, but we did it."

Champions. Again.

CONTENTS

BOOK STAFF

Editor Reid Laymance
Designer Rena Anderson Sokolow
Photo editor Jim Wilson
Copy editor Mike Kilduff
Photo Research Theresa Grenier
Special Thanks Alex Teng

PANTHERS

32-29

HOUSTON

FEBRUARY 1
2004

INDOORS

All over again

by DAN SHAUGHNESSY

Yogi Berra would have called it, "Deja vu all over again."

It was all so familiar . . . Adam Vinatieri kicking the game-winner . . . quarterback Tom Brady winning the Most Valuable Player Award . . . coach Bill Belichick and owner Bob Kraft hoisting the Vince Lombardi Trophy while Patriot players hugged and brushed confetti off one another. All of these things happened two years ago when the Patriots upset the St. Louis Rams in New Orleans.

After the Patriots had beaten Carolina, 32-29, in Houston for their second Super Bowl in three years, Kraft told the crowd, "Fifty-three players, 17 coaches, a head coach—the heart and soul of our team showed us what the concept of team is all about."

FIRST DOWNS		RUSHING YARDS	PASSING YARDS	TURNOVERS
NE 29	CAR 17	127 92	354 295	1 1

IT'S UP
Adam Vinatieri's 41-yard field goal was right down the middle and good to give the Patriots the win with four seconds left.

SACKS	PENALTIES	TIME OF POSSESSION	OPPONENTS RECORD
4 0	8 12	38:58 21:02	17-2 14-6

FUMBLE
Mike Vrabel, who
would later score
on offense,
knocks the ball
out of Carolina
quarterback Jake
Delhomme's
hands.

Championships are like children—you love each one equally. But the manner in which the 2003-04 Patriots went about their business makes this title a slightly favored son. The Patriots finished the season with 15 consecutive wins, went 10-0 against winning teams, and went 10 weeks without trailing in a game before the Panthers put them on the ropes at Reliant Stadium.

As ever, Brady was Joe Montana-cool under pressure. With the game tied and a little more than a minute to play, he moved the Patriots 37 yards in six plays, setting up Vinatieri's 41-yard kick for the win with four seconds left. The clutch kicker had missed a 31-yard chip shot, and had another attempt blocked, but his final boot was straight and true.

"Maybe a little deja vu of two years ago," said Vinatieri. "The fellows moved the ball downfield and we had the opportunity to win it again. This never gets old. With this type of venue and the pressure on, it's never easy, but you try to block all the external things out and kick it. I'll cherish this for a long time."

Meanwhile, what's left for Brady? John Kerry's running mate? First man on Mars? Starting pitcher for the Red Sox when they finally win a World Series? The 26-year-old golden child becomes the youngest two-time Super Bowl-winning quarterback and one of only four players to win the MVP Award twice. He completed 32 of 48 passes for 354 yards and three touchdowns. He is 6-0 lifetime in playoff games.

"The guys made some great catches there on that last drive," said Brady. "And Adam drove that sucker right down the middle to win it. What a game. Fitting for the Super Bowl, I guess."

When the Patriots trailed for the first time since before Thanksgiving, Brady moved them 68 yards on 11 plays and regained the lead with a 1-yard touchdown pass to linebacker Mike Vrabel. When the Panthers roared back to tie the game, Brady responded again.

"It was an awesome year," said Belichick. "I can't say enough about the players. We finished the game with two backup safeties. That's the way it's been all year."

So now it's Groundhog Day, where the scene keeps repeating itself, much like in the Bill Murray movie, but there's no one left to beat. Too bad. Patriots fans surely would embrace six more weeks of football. In the wake of the coldest January since 1888, and the most disappointing Red Sox finish since 1986, New England needed a lift, and the Patriots delivered with a season for the ages.

In the end, the Super Bowl win was like so many others in this magical Patriots season. The Patriots failed to overwhelm their opponents, relied on strong defense, got contributions from the entire roster, and left it to Brady and Vinatieri to come through at the finish. The fact that New England's final touchdown pass was caught by a linebacker tells you much of what you need to know about this team.

By any measure, these Patriots go into the books as one of the best and most beloved Boston sports teams of the last 100 years. Not since the Larry Bird Celtics of 1984 and '86 has a local team won two championships in three seasons. The Bruins last did it in 1970 and '72 and the Red Sox haven't turned the trick since 1916 and '18.

The 2003-04 Patriots featured one of the best defenses in league history, used 42 different starters, had only two Pro Bowlers, and took pride in selflessness and interchangeable parts. At times, it looked as if they had 11 coaches on the field. They transformed their two-year-old stadium into the happiest place on earth.

The camaraderie of the Patriots was evident at the start again. Troy Brown, the senior Patriot in continuous service, led the AFC champions onto the field. And as they did two years ago, the Patriots poured out of their tunnel en masse—a show of unity that was copied by the Panthers. It was clear at this moment that the Super Bowl would be like another home game for Belichick's team. Patriot Nation made its presence felt and there were moments when Reliant Stadium sounded like the football theater off Route 1 in Foxborough.

It started out like a World Cup game and was still 0-0 with a little more than three minutes to play in the first half. But Brady threw a pair of touchdown passes in the final three minutes and Carolina's Jake Delhomme started to move his team and New England led, 14-10, at intermission.

After a ribald halftime show featuring Janet Jackson, play was interrupted briefly when a streaker managed to line up with the Panthers for the opening kickoff. He was chased by authorities and eventually brought down when Patriots linebacker Matt Chatham put a shoulder into him. Needless to say, Belichick was not amused.

It got wild again after a scoreless third quarter. The teams traded touchdowns early in the fourth. After a Brady interception, the Panthers struck again on the longest play from scrimmage in Super Bowl history, an 85-yard pass from Delhomme to Muhsin Muhammad. Carolina led, 22-21, with 6:53 left.

Brady went to work and it was madness the rest of the way. As always, the Patriots came through in the clutch.

No doubt there will be whispers of "dynasty." The well-managed, brilliantly coached Patriots are in position to make it back to the national stage in Jacksonville next year.

THE LEGACY

Simply the best

by MICHAEL HOLLEY

IT IS NOW OK TO PLACE THE NEW ENGLAND Patriots in a historical sentence that few teams are able to utter. You can call them one of the greatest teams of all time, and you can say it without apologizing or blinking or giving a monologue on this era of free agency.

The Patriots are great. Swallow it straight, with no chaser.

A few things became obvious when the Patriots won Super Bowl XXXVIII, 32-29 over the Carolina Panthers:

Adam Vinatieri is one of the best clutch athletes New England sports fans have ever seen. We're not just talking about clutch kickers or clutch football players. We're talking athletes, regardless of the sport and regardless of the decade.

Vinatieri and his teammates can start their own drama club.

Tom Brady has played in two Super Bowls, has led two winning drives in the final 90 seconds, and has to make room for another MVP Cadillac in his Quincy, Mass., garage.

Bill Belichick is the top head coach in the NFL, Scott Pioli is the league's leading personnel man, and Robert Kraft is the most exceptional of Paul Tagliabue's 32 owners.

And, of course, there is this: A team that wins 15 consecutive games has to be considered one of the finest in the history of the league.

"It's us and it's the [undefeated] 1972 Dolphins," Patriots vice chairman Jonathan Kraft said on the floor of Reliant Stadium. He was holding the Lombardi Trophy high above his head when he said it. The trophy had long lost its glitter because it was covered with fingerprints. They were the fingerprints of players, coaches, medical staff, video staff, families, and friends.

That has always been the beauty of this Patriots team. It was brilliantly built, built in such a way that one man cannot disrupt the system. It was built with corny words—spirit and soul and integrity—in mind as well.

"The message," Belichick said, "is that you can do this the right way. You can win with players who are not looking to promote themselves and be selfish. You can win with people who care about the team first."

A lot of coaches say that, but they say it with a trace of fantasy. Belichick and Pioli have seen it happen twice in the past three seasons.

"Here's all you have to know about our team," Belichick said. "We won all those games in a row, and not one person wants to take credit for it. Not one guy. Brady credits the offensive line. The coaches credit the players. Ty [Law] got three interceptions in the AFC Championship game, and he says the pressure from the defensive line made it possible.

"How cool is that?"

Probably as cool as Brady in the fourth quarter last night. The Patriots were leading, 21-16, and were one score from putting the Panthers in a difficult position. On third down at the Carolina 9, Brady threw a pass intended for Christian Fauria. It was intercepted. Carolina turned the turnover into a touchdown that put the Panthers ahead, 22-21.

Then Brady came back with a touchdown to Mike Vrabel—Mike Vrabel!—and watched Kevin Faulk complete the 2-point conversion. Carolina responded with a touchdown, and then Brady again put Vinatieri in position to make a winning kick.

"I don't know if we're the greatest or not," Law said. "But I'll tell you what we'll do. We'll compete against any team."

No, they don't scare you. They don't have steel coming out of their chests as the Steelers of the 1970s did. They didn't win all their games like the Dolphins of '72. Belichick doesn't stalk the sideline like Vince Lombardi, shouting out instructions under the lid of a fedora.

But this team is resourceful. It can win games with defense and it can win by topping 30 points. It can win in nasty conditions, such as the divisional playoff over Tennessee and the AFC East clincher over Miami. It can win ugly games (9-3 over Cleveland, 17-6 over the New York Giants), and it can win games that just may be considered the most thrilling in league history.

The Patriots' victory over the Rams in Super Bowl XXXVI was like that. So was their win over the Panthers. They had plenty to talk about as they partied at the Intercontinental Hotel in Houston after the game. The face of the organization had a collective smile.

The Panthers? It must be said that the losing team was outstanding in this game. The people of the Carolinas should be proud of the tough team that represents them. If the Patriots are truly a dynasty, and it appears that they are, they will know that the Panthers will be a likely Super Bowl dance partner for the next five years.

New England, though, was just a little better and a little tougher. And that's the way the Patri-

ots played all season. They were fallible enough to make every team believe it had a chance. They were skilled and creative enough to handle every tough situation.

Even a source as unlikely as rapper Snoop Dogg found that out before the Patriots' Saturday practice. Snoop, a guest of Willie McGinest's, was taking pictures with several Patriots. When he saw Belichick, Snoop was surprised to hear the coach's first words.

"Hey," Belichick said. "Gin and juice, right?"

That's a reference to one of the rapper's songs. Who knew Belichick was familiar with it? Then again, who knew that all of New England would be presented with a team like this?

BIG CATCH
Deion Branch led the Patriots with 10 receptions for 143 yards, including this one to set up a score.

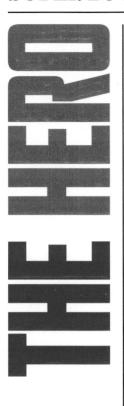

The sure thing

by JACKIE MAC MULLAN

THERE ARE VERY FEW THINGS IN LIFE THAT Patriots linebacker Mike Vrabel is absolutely, positively certain about.

Kicker Adam Vinatieri is one of them.

"I was sure he'd make it," said Vrabel, rubbing his son Tyler's head in the afterglow of his team's second Super Bowl victory in three years. "Adam is like Deion Sanders. If he ever messes up, you just know he's going to make sure he'll get the next one.

"It's just unbelievable what he's done. The guy is so deserving of whatever comes his way. He is the best clutch kicker ever, in the history of this league. When he was lining up for that kick, I couldn't even see the goal post, there were so many flashbulbs going off. I would have needed a visor to kick it."

Vinatieri won Super Bowl XXXVIII for the Patriots in the final seconds without wearing anything on his head. He did, however, put on longer spikes at halftime, after a recently sprayed field proved to be a little slicker than he'd like. He would never use that as an excuse for the unthinkable happening in the opening drive. The Patriots got into the habit of scoring the very first time they had the ball, and it appeared they would do the same against a stingy Carolina defense.

Quarterback Tom Brady coaxed his offensive unit down to the 18-yard line, and then it was the kicker's turn. All Vinatieri had to do was line up and boot a 31-yard field goal, which is about as routine for him as lacing up his spikes. But as soon as he kicked it, he knew. Wide right.

"I don't know," mused Vinatieri. "That first one, probably I was a little excited. I probably

was a little too fast."

He had always been automatic, particularly during that magical Super Bowl season two years ago, when he kicked five game-winning field goals. The most famous play of his marvelous career—the kick in the snow to eliminate the Oakland Raiders—vaulted him to stardom. It didn't hurt, of course, that when Super Bowl XXXVI ticked down to the final seconds, he lined up and calmly knocked a 48-yard field goal through the uprights to upend the heavily favored St. Louis Rams.

And, so, we got used to expecting him to be perfect—or nearly so. Last year, when the team collectively experienced a Super letdown, Vinatieri was better than ever, successful on 90 percent (27 of 30) of his kicks. It was the highest percentage in the NFL, and as the Patriots staff looked to the future, it never occurred to them to worry about their kicker.

But this season was a trying one for Vinatieri. He struggled with back problems he wasn't supposed to talk about. He struggled with a merry-go-round of snappers and holders, something he wasn't supposed to talk about either. He is a team player, an eternal optimist, and he never—ever—let on to the hordes of media that tromped past his locker how frustrated he was at times. He converted only 25 of 34 field goals in the regular season. He—horrors!—actually missed an extra point.

He was able to wipe the numbers clean each week because he lives by the kicker's mentality: whatever just happened, forget it.

"You don't ever want to ever think about the last kick, good or bad," Vinatieri said. "The only

one you should ever care about is the one in front of you."

So fine. Forget about missing that 31-yarder in the first quarter last night. Forget about the 36-yard attempt that was blocked by Carolina's Shane Burton with six minutes left until halftime.

But wait a minute. Deion Sanders would never forget that. He'd dwell on them until he got himself good and ticked off, and marched back on the field to right his wrongs. He would seep in his own failure until he left himself no choice but to succeed the next time out.

"Well, OK, yeah," Vinatieri acknowledged. "I'm as competitive as anybody. It would be like a receiver dropping the ball, and making sure he got the next one, or a defender blowing a coverage, and making a play the next time. I'm just glad my teammates have that kind of confidence in me."

The kicker has a tricky role on a football team. He does a lot of waiting around, often feeling, as Vinatieri has confessed in the past, a bit disconnected from the team. But when your time comes, you become the most important player on the field. It is a responsibility that Vinatieri has never feared, only craved.

And so he waited, and hoped for another chance. When Carolina quarterback Jake Delhomme's 85-yard bomb to Muhsin Muhammad gave the Panthers a 22-21 lead with 6:53 left, Vinatieri began preparing for a role in the responding drive. That was not necessary when Tom Brady found Vrabel in the end zone. But there was Delhomme again, connecting with veteran Ricky Proehl, and the score was tied, 29-29.

Vinatieri looked up at the scoreboard, and smiled. There was 1:08 left on the clock.

"Even if you ever give us any time, look out," he said.

His quarterback did what he does best: he managed the team down the field. Brady got the ball to the 23-yard line, leaving Vinatieri eight seconds and 41 yards to win it. As he ran onto the field, he surveyed Reliant Stadium, filled with 71,525 screaming fans, and he felt . . . nothing.

Nothing but calm.

"I had no doubt," said linebacker Tedy Bruschi. "I've seen him make kick after kick after kick after kick. How could anyone doubt him?"

As the ball sailed through the uprights, and Vinatieri was mobbed by his teammates (again), poised to be the Super Bowl hero (again), all the misses of a long, long season went poof, like the flashbulbs exploding around him.

He is the best clutch kicker in the business. Try and tell his teammates differently.

"It never gets old," said Vinatieri, when asked how he felt. "It never gets old."

Two Super Bowls. Two winning kicks. That's something no kicker should ever forget.

YEAH!
Adam Vinatieri
has a moment
alone to savor
his winning
field goal.

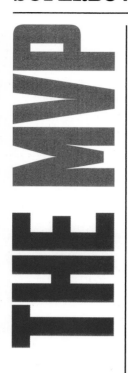

Mr. Cool

by KEVIN PAUL DUPONT

IT WASN'T AS IF A TATTERED SCRIPT FELL FROM the Reliant Stadium roof, a remnant from New Orleans two Super Bowls ago. But as the final moments played out, Carolina receiver Ricky Proehl felt as if he had seen it all before, the ending playing "Brady going down the field," said Proehl, who two years ago was a member of the St. Louis Rams club that was stunned by New England in the Super Bowl. "The same thing . . . and Vinatieri kicked the field goal. When it was over, I had the sick feeling again."

Cool, calm, and seemingly inflappable, Brady further burnished his image as a clutch postseason performer, connecting on 32 of 48 passes, good for 354 yards and three touchdowns, and pacing the Patriots to a come-from-behind 32-29 Super Bowl victory over the defensively-tenacious Panthers.

The 26-year-old Brady, with only 68 seconds remaining in regulation, once again marched his squad downfield. Over the next 59 seconds, the Patriots chewed up 37 yards in six plays, bringing the ball to the Carolina 23. Over on the sideline, Proehl's stomach was beginning to flip.

"When we need 'em, they cash in," said Deion Branch, reflecting on whether Brady or Vinatieri was the calmest under pressure. "Both of 'em [are the same]. The coaches always say, 'When your number's called, you've got to cash in.'"

Brady further cashed in after the win when he was named the MVP, winning a Cadillac XLR. He also was named the MVP two years ago.

Branch and Brady tried to connect to open the winning drive, but the result was the last of Brady's 16 incompletions. Then came a 13-yard pass to Troy Brown, followed by another to Brown for 20 more, which was nullified for offensive pass interference. Brown redeemed himself with a 13-yard catch on the next snap. The next two plays had Brady first hitting Daniel Graham for 4 more yards, and then a 17-yard hookup wiith Branch. The ball was at the Carolina 23, and Vinatieri was on his way in from the sideline.

"I was just trying to get it a little closer there to shorten the field goal," said Branch. "They had a short coverage there, because they figured out what we were doing. My thought there is, if I can score, I try to score, but I just want to get as close for Adam as I can."

Brady, his helmet off, watched from the sideline as Vinatieri ripped through the ball with his right foot. It couldn't have been more than 10 feet into flight when Vinatieri, who earlier missed a chip shot and had another attempt blocked, raised a clenched right fist. He knew where it was going, and he knew the Patriots were going home winners.

"Adam drilled it right down the middle to win it," said a beaming Brady, sounding more California mellow than East Coast jubilant at the postgame podium. "What a game. What a game. Fitting for a Super Bowl, I guess."

The Patriots had not trailed since last being in Houston Nov. 23. But neither Brady nor anyone else on the New England sideline so much as flinched under the pressure.

"We've been down before," he said. "We just don't lose composure."

If not for the winning drive, Brady risked his signature moment of the night being his pass, intended for Christian Fauria with 7:48 remaining in the fourth, that Reggie Howard picked off in the end zone and ran back to the 10. Four plays later, Jake Delhomme threw an 85-yard touchdown pass to Muhsin Muhammad, ultimately lifting the Panthers to the 22-21 lead.

Flustered? Who, Brady?

"That's what happens in the Super Bowl, you know?" said Brady. "They make great plays, too."

There is a confidence in the Patriots, said Brady, in which they believe they can "win anything."

"But to win this, the way we did it," he added. "It's just unbelievable the way we did it." Two Super Bowls. A pair of victories. Matching MVPs. The inevitable comparisons to former 49ers great Joe Montana.

"I said all week, he's the benchmark for quarterbacks in the league," said Brady, gingerly sidestepping undesired pressure one last time. "This is only my fourth year, and in no way am I close to that. Hopefully one day I'm on that level, but not yet."

REPEAT
Tom Brady won the Super Bowl's MVP award for a second time.

THE DRIVE

Like clockwork

by JOHN POWERS

THIS TEAM GENUFLECTS TO NOBODY. NOT IF there's still time on the clock and a championship trophy waiting at the other end of the field. The Patriots did not take a knee, did not play for overtime when they shocked the Rams to win their first Super Bowl two years ago. They were not going to take a knee against the Panthers, not with 68 seconds left to them, not with only a few stripes to cover to get Adam Vinatieri within range. And the Carolina Panthers knew it.

"Play to win," said Carolina defensive tackle Brentson Buckner, after Vinatieri's magic right foot had broken the Panthers' hearts. "That's what you do. You play to win. You don't play to go into overtime. They did what they needed to do."

There was less time on this final drive than there was against St. Louis, when quarterback Tom Brady had 1:30 to work with. But there also was less real estate to cover after New England got the ball on its own 40 after Carolina had scored to tie the game at 29.

"We had 1:08 and three timeouts," said offensive coordinator Charlie Weis. "That made the play calls a little easier, especially when [John Kasay's] kickoff went out of bounds. Instead of having to go 40 or 50 yards, we only had to go 30 to where we know Adam has a chance at it."

Problem was, after three plays and 24 seconds, the Patriots had moved only 3 yards, after a questionable offensive pass interference call on receiver Troy Brown brought the ball back to the 43 instead of putting it on the Panthers' 27.

Still, the Carolina front four hadn't been getting to Brady, who was sitting patiently in the shotgun as his underappreciated offensive line held off Julius Peppers and friends all night. Now, he calmly picked the Panthers' secondary apart.

Brady went right back to Brown on first and 20

for 13 yards, threading the ball between linebacker Will Witherspoon and cornerback Terry Cousin. "We were in a zone," said Panthers safety Mike Minter, "and they put the ball right in the perfect spot."

Twenty seconds left now, second and 7 with the ball on the Carolina 44 and Vinatieri warming up his leg on the sideline. Here was Brady throwing again, this time a 4-yarder to tight end Daniel Graham to the 40 a second timeout.

Now came the play, on third and 3, that went for Carolina's throat with 14 seconds left. "It was a combo route with Brown and Deion Branch," Weis said. And it caught the Panthers guessing wrong.

Would Brady look for Brown quickly on the shallow route for the first down and maybe a bit more? Or would he risk a longer throw that would put them within field goal range? "They bit on the shallow route," said Weis, "and Deion was open up top, and Brady hit him the way he always does."

Brady had been outgaming the Panthers for most of the evening. As soon as he saw their coverage, he figured a ball to Branch for 17 yards to the 23 was the bull's-eye call.

"I think we had the perfect play called for that coverage," Brady said. "We were really anticipating what they were going to do and Deion ran a great route. I just laid it up there for him and he made a great catch. And it gave us just enough time to call a timeout, and then Adam to run on the field."

Nine seconds left now, which is an eternity for this team. "If you ever give us any time," mused Vinatieri, "look out." The Panthers called a timeout to ice him, but they were merely crossing their fingers.

Vinatieri had only missed four of his 35 previ-

ous indoor attempts, but all of them had come in-side Reliant Stadium. The first had missed just wide. The second had been blocked by massive defensive tackle Shane Burton.

But the Panthers, who'd seen the film clip of Vinatieri's previous Super Bowl winner a million times, weren't counting on him missing a second time. Not from 41 yards in the middle of the field.

"I wasn't thinking about him missing," said defensive end Mike Rucker. "I was thinking about us blocking it. But we just weren't able to get that one."

Not even close. Vinatieri drilled the ball right down Main Street and halfway to downtown, and the Patriots had won their second ring in three years.

"It never gets old," Vinatieri declared. "It never, ever gets old."

FOCUS
Tom Brady lines up to hit Deion Branch with the pass to set up the winning field goal.

CELEBRATE
Rodney Harrison, his arm in a sling, takes in his first championship with the Patriots.

AFC CHAMPIONSHIP

COLTS

FOXBOROUGH

24-14

JANUARY 18
2003

32 DEGREES
SNOWING

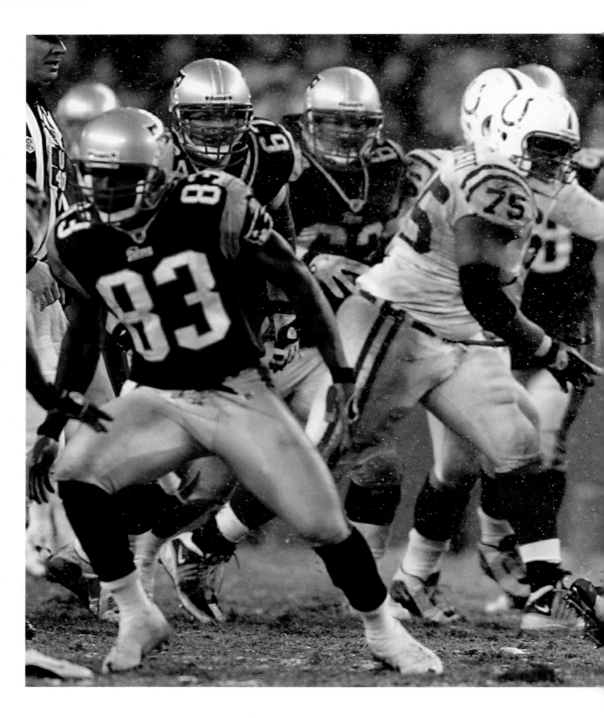

Crowning moment

by DAN SHAUGHNESSY

FIRST DOWNS	RUSHING YARDS	PASSING YARDS	TURNOVERS
NE 20 | 21 IND	112 | 98	237 | 208	2 | 5

GROUND GAIN
Antowain Smith's
100 yards rushing
helped the
Patriots run
down the Colts.

IN THE END, IT WAS MORE CELEBRATION THAN
contest, more coronation than competition.

The New England Patriots are going to the Super Bowl for the fourth time in franchise history, the second time in three years: New England vs. the Carolina Panthers in Super Bowl

XXXVIII at Reliant Stadium in Houston.

In a final, flurried, fun-filled afternoon at Gillette Stadium, the Patriots won their 14th consecutive game, a 24-14 dismantling of the Indianapolis Colts in the AFC Championship game. There was little artistic about the win, but

SACKS	PENALTIES	TIME OF POSSESSION	RECORD
4│0	3│4	32:14│27:46	16-2│14-5

the Patriots again demonstrated that theirs is the best defense in the NFL.

"To win 14 in a row is unbelievable," said ever-blessed quarterback Tom Brady. "Who does that? Nobody does that. Still, the goal really hasn't been achieved if we don't get 15. Then it's all for naught . . . But I'm proud to be quarterback of a team that's going to the Super Bowl two times in three years."

Brady and the Patriots won the 2002 Super Bowl in New Orleans against the Rams, one of the epic upsets in football history. This time, New England will be favored. Bill Belichick's 16-2 team is the best team in franchise history, and by closing with 15 straight wins could go down as one of the best in the annals of the NFL.

Just look at what happened. Peyton Manning and Co. came to Foxborough on the heels of two of the greatest offensive performances in play-off lore, then limped out of Gillette with an acute case of Mad Colt Disease. Indianapolis turned the ball over five times and bumbled a punt attempt (errant snap) into a safety. The previously indomitable Manning was intercepted four times — thrice by Ty Law — completed fewer than half of his passes, and didn't get his

team on the scoreboard until the third quarter.

"The real thrill was being able to do it in front of our fans," said Patriots owner, Bob Kraft – the most popular and successful Boston pro sports owner since Walter Brown steered the Bill Russell Celtics. "The fans are the 12th man that helped us go 12-0 [including the exhibition season] at home."

Upon accepting the Lamar Hunt trophy, signifying AFC supremacy, Kraft told the lingering 68,000, "We want you all down there in Houston and let's bring that trophy back."

With so many veterans of Super Bowl XXXVI still around, the Patriots did not go overboard in celebration (remember the Red Sox and that ridiculous wild-card clincher?). They donned AFC champion hats and T-shirts, but there were no champagne baths in the winner's locker room.

"It's just another game for us in a way," said All-Pro defensive end Richard Seymour. "It's a step on the way to our ultimate goal."

They will miss the zany masses who filled the Razor 12 times. In the second year of the stadium's existence, the Patriots' crib became the toughest place to win. Fans braved traffic, heat,

rain, snow, 3-foot drifts, parking nightmares, and wind chill temperatures of 10-below zero. None of it mattered. They came early, stayed late, and shook down the thunder every time the PA played Gary Glitter's Rock 'n' Roll Part 2. Sixty-eight thousand 12th men and women. Not bad.

The final home game could not have started in better fashion for New England. With friendly flakes falling, the Patriots took the opening kiczkoff and marched 65 yards in 13 plays, scoring on a 7-yard touchdown pass from Brady to David Givens. The Patriots led, 7-0, and just as important, almost half of the first quarter was already over.

Manning moved the Colts to the New England 7-yard line, then was intercepted in the end zone by Rodney Harrison. It was a terrible throw. It was also Manning's first interception of the 2004 playoffs. He had eight touchdown passes and no picks in the indomitable victories over Denver and Kansas City.

A 31-yard Adam Vinatieri field goal made it 10-0 early in the second, Then came the first and most spectacular of Law's three interceptions. Think Carl Yastrzemski, April of '67, ninth inning, grabbing Tom Tresh's liner to deep left in Billy Rohr's no-hit bid. A 25-yard field goal followed and it was 13-0. At that point, the Colts' only two possessions had both ended with interceptions.

Indy's next offensive series resulted in the Colts lining up for their first punt of the playoffs. Colt long snapper Justin Snow hiked the ball over Hunter Smith's head. The rusty punter gave chase and booted the ball across the opposite goal line. The result of the chaos was a Patriot saftey and a 15-0 lead.

The Colts gave the Patriots a couple of scares in the second half, but any time things got tight, the New England defense did the job.

So like the Kennedys in Massachusestts, the Patriots went undeated in their home state. And now there's only one game left. Indoors – without all the trappings of home.

"I don't think we're going to have to worry about the snow or 20-below wind chills or anything like that," said Vinatieri, the undisputed king of bad-weather kickers.

No more snow. No more cold. No more Gillette.

Just the Super Bowl. The final crowning for the best football team New England ever has known.

BOB KRAFT "The fans are the 12th man that help us go 12-0 at home."

TITANS

FOXBOROUGH

17-14

JANUARY 10
2004

4 DEGREES
WINDY

Shivering heights

by MICHAEL SMITH

GIVE HIM CREDIT. HE CALLED IT. BILL Belichick predicted that the AFC divisional play-off game at Gillette Stadium against the Tennessee Titans would be the Patriots' toughest game of the season. It sounded like a cliche when he said it. But Belichick couldn't have been more accurate.

Playing in the coldest game in franchise history (4 degrees, minus-10 windchill at kickoff), the top-seeded Patriots held on for a 17-14 win over the wild-card Titans. Adam Vinatieri, who had missed a 44-yard field goal in the first quarter, gave New England its 13th straight win with a 46-yarder with 4 minutes 6 seconds to play.

The Titans made it interesting on their last possession, driving 36 yards to New England's 40 before self-destructing after the two-minute warning. First, Tennessee was penalized 10 yards for intentional grounding by Steve McNair. Guard Benji Olson's holding penalty pushed the Titans back another 10 yards and put them in a third-and-22 situation.

McNair threw 10 yards to Drew Bennett on third down. On fourth and 12 from New England's 43, Rodney Harrison's blitz forced McNair to throw up a jump ball to Bennett, who bobbled it and had it knocked away by Asante Samuel.

"It was everything we expected of this game," Belichick said. "All their key players played well. We were fortunate to make more plays than Tennessee did."

"It was one of the more intense games I've played in," Harrison said.

The Patriots gained 297 yards to the Titans' 284. McNair played like a co-MVP, completing 18 of 26 passes for 210 yards. But, as it has all season, New England's defense stiffened when it had to. "It was our season," Harrison said. "We had let them go downfield, and enough was enough. We challenged them. We stepped up and said if they're going to beat us, they're going to beat us. You can't let him sit back there and

sling the ball. We decided to try something different and give him a different look."

After the game the Patriots did not have the look of a team that was a win away from the Super Bowl. "We're not jumping for joy in here," Tedy Bruschi said. "We know what we want to do. We're just one step closer."

"We're not looking at the Super Bowl. We're looking at one game at a time," said Harrison, repeating what has become a familiar refrain. "You don't see guys jumping around. We're focused."

Titans guard Zach Piller was not impressed, even after the Patriots had beaten the Titans for a second time this season. "Everyone was talking about their defense," Piller said. "I thought it sucked. It'd be a shock to me if they were holding the trophy at the end of all of this. . . . I will not leave this stadium thinking we got beat by a better team. I think that that team is not a very good team and it sickens me that we lost to them. It just wasn't our day."

The Titans took their first possession of the second half and marched 70 yards in 11 plays, tying the game on Steve McNair's 11-yard collaboration with Derrick Mason. The drive took 7:47 and included a 30-yard completion from McNair to Tyrone Calico. On the touchdown, Mason took McNair's short pass, slipped the attempted tackle of Asante Samuel, and leaped over Tyrone Poole and the pylon.

New England hadn't committed any major errors until tight end Daniel Graham fumbled (Kevin Carter forced it) and the Titans' Carlos Hall recovered near midfield. But the Patriots' defense didn't budge, forcing Tennessee into a three and out. Credit Willie McGinest for the stop; he blew up an attempted screen to Frank Wycheck, tackling the tight end for a 10-yard loss on first down.

That set the stage for the fourth quarter and more heroics from Vinatieri and the defense.

FIRST DOWNS	RUSHING YARDS	PASSING YARDS	TURNOVERS
NE 18 | 16 TEN	96 | 84	201 | 200	1 | 1

ON TARGET
From the hold of Ken Walter,
Adam Vinatieri's 46-yard
field goal is true to beat the
Titans in the fourth quarter.

SACKS	PENALTIES	TIME OF POSSESSION	RECORD
4 0	2 9	28:02 31:58	15-2 13-5

THE GAMES

A season of focus

by JOHN POWERS

January is the month of both anticipation and reflection, named after the two-faced Roman god who looked both forward and backward. If Janus played for the Patriots, though, he'd be wearing blinkers. In Bill Belichick's myopic universe, December never happened and February is a century away.

"Everybody is 0-0 now," Belichick said, as soon as the regular season ended. "We all know what it is. Lose, and you are out. Win, and you keep going. That is it.

New England's achievements in the regular season were impressive and undeniable—a franchise-record 14 victories, the last 12 in a row. A perfect home record. The best defense in club history.

"It doesn't matter how you got here," said Belichick. "Whether you won them in a row, didn't win them in a row, however it happened."

The Patriots got here by living exclusively in the moment, by ignoring previous and future Sundays, by using the players available to them, by accepting—and adjusting to—conditions as they found them, and by expecting to win every game by whatever means necessary.

RUSHING OFFENSE	PASSING OFFENSE	SCORING OFFENSE	TURNOVER RATIO
100.4 (27th)	214.5 (9th)	348 (12th)	+17 (2d)

TOM TERRIFIC
Quarterback Tom Brady made all the plays down the stretch for the streaking Patriots.

RUSHING DEFENSE	PASSING DEFENSE	SCORING DEFENSE	PENALTIES
89.6 (4th)	202 (15th)	238 (1st)	111 (22st)

It's not like we're Pavlov's dogs or anything," mused linebacker Ted Johnson. "But we're conditioned to prepare a certain way."

That was how Belichick's charges smacked down Philadelphia after losing to Buffalo in the worst opening-game defeatin franchise history, how they knocked off Tennessee after losing to Washington.

That was how the Patriots smothered the Giants with nine starters missing, how they ended the Miami jinx, how they outfoxed Denver, outlasted Houston, and outpointed Indianapolis. "New England just outcoached, outpersonneled, and outplayed everybody," conceded Tom Donahoe, Buffalo's president and general manager.

Nobody was saying that after the Bills destroyed New England, 31-0, in Game 1, just days after star safety Lawyer Milloy went from teammate to opponent. The Patriots were pathetic on defense in their debut, punchless on offense. "This wasn't us today," acknowledged linebacker Mike Vrabel.

Were they distracted by the Milloy changeover? Poorly prepared? Overrated? Did they hate their coach, as ESPN commentator Tom Jackson later opined? "There is a lot of football left to be played," observed Belichick, who said on that Sunday that he wasn't looking past Monday. "It is short-term, and it is day-by-day."

Game 2 would be against a different team in a different place with a different game plan. The Eagles eventually won their division, but that day they were missing half of their secondary.

So quarterback Tom Brady threw three play-action touchdown passes, two to tight end Christian Fauria, the defense harassed Donovan McNabb into a brutal performance (18 of 46 for 186 yards with no touchdowns, eight sacks, and two interceptions, one for a touchdown by Tedy Bruschi) and New England left the field a 31-10 victor.

It's already forgotten
One Sunday had nothing to do with the next. That was the Belichick credo. What he hated most about his job, he would say, was returning to the locker room at 4 o'clock after a loss, a week's preparation gone for naught. But at 4:01, the next Sunday began, with another chance for victory.

"Every game we've played since I've been here, we felt like we were going to win," Belichick said. "We obviously didn't win all of them, but that's how we felt going in."

Which is why the 20-17 loss at Washington in Game 4—the last defeat of the regular season—rankled. The squad was missing five offensive and four defensive starters that day, and Brady's throwing shoulder and elbow were hurting. But the players still expected to prevail.

"We should have won the game," said Bruschi, after the Patriots had climbed out of a 20-3 hole and tried a fourth-down pass in the final minute instead of going for a tying field goal. "To say it was a moral victory, you're asking me to settle, and I won't. I won't settle for any loss."

Even if nearly half of the lineup was on crutches. Football is a smashmouth sport and broken bones and ripped ligaments are routine and always will be. "The game is going to move on," said safety Rodney Harrison.

And the rules still call for 11 men on the field, whether or not they'd expected to be there. "We're a 53-man roster," said guard Joe Andruzzi. "Nobody's here to collect a backup-role check. If someone goes down, you have to be able to step up."

With its regulars missing 103 games with injuries, New England plugged in 42 different starters and used the same lineup for consecutive games only once. The defense, which lost one linebacker (Rosevelt Colvin) for the season, another (Johnson) for eight games, and nose tackle Ted Washington for six more, switched from a 3-4 scheme to a 4-3, then back again five times.

"Right now, we're just willing ourselves," said cornerback Tyrone Poole, after the Patriots had survived a wet and grimy wrangle with the Giants in Game 6.

They still were minus nine starters. They managed just 29 yards in the first half and eight pass completions for the game. They converted just 1 of 11 third downs and committed 10 penalties. Yet they still won, 17-6, because the defense made four interceptions and Matt Chatham returned a fumble 38 yards for a touchdown. "Man, that was a great win for our football team," declared Belichick.

The greatest, though, came the following week at Miami, where New England had never won a game in September or October (as in 0-13). "We've got to get those guys," vowed guard Damien Woody. "They beat the crap out of us. It's been ugly games down there ever since I came here."

With two minutes left in regulation and Dolphins kicker Olindo Mare setting up for a 35-yard field goal, the Patriots appeared squelched again. Mare had only had two of 201 career attempts blocked. "What are the chances?" asked defensive lineman Richard Seymour, after he'd batted the ball away to force overtime.

Then, after losing the coin toss, New England shrewdly chose to defend the west end of Pro Player Stadium, where the baseball infield was, to force Mare to kick on dirt.

After Mare missed right, Brady promptly lofted an 82-yard touchdown pass to Troy Brown for the 19-13 victory that made both the Patriots and their fans believe that anything was possible. "If you look back," said center Dan Koppen, "that was the turning point for this team."

The starters would vary, the game plans change, but week after week, there was a victory. Almost all of them were close—11 straight times, New England won by two touchdowns or less, an NFL record. And most went down to the final minutes. "We're just going to play it out and when 60 minutes is up, we'll see how it ends," said Woody, after his mates had subdued Cleveland, 9-3. "See who's the last one standing."

The triumphs often were grinding and graceless, like the 12-0 throttlings of Dallas and Miami. But Belichick didn't care about style points, as long as the day ended in a W. "It's hard to win in this league," he said. "However you can win, you better be happy about it."

Even if it meant clanging a snap off the goal post for an intentional safety, as Lonie Paxton did in Denver with the Patriots trailing by a point with less than three minutes to play and backed up against their end zone.

After Ken Walter's free kick chased the Broncos back to their 15 and the defense forced them three-and-out, Brady threw an 18-yard touchdown pass to David Givens with 30 seconds left for a 30-26 victory. "It was a horrible knife in the guts for Denver," Hunter S. Thompson observed on ESPN.com.

It was all about execution under pressure, Belichick said. The Patriots beat Houston in overtime by stopping the Texans three times, then kicking a field goal with 41 seconds to play. Then, after squandering a three-touchdown lead in the second half, they slammed the door on the Colts by stacking them up three times at the 1-yard-line with less than 25 seconds to play.

"To be the best, you've got to stop the best," said linebacker Willie McGinest, after he'd lassoed Edgerrin James on fourth down. "And we did that."

Their defense (ranked seventh) and offense (17th) weren't at the top of the NFL statistical page and they only had two players (Seymour and cornerback Ty Law) chosen for the Pro Bowl.

But the Patriots won those 14 games by using their entire roster and by focusing on the statistics that produce victories—points allowed (a league-low 14.9, a franchise record), a turnover differential of plus-17 (another franchise record), an NFL-high six defensive touchdowns, and red-zone scoring (42 of 50, 22 of them touchdowns).

Mostly, though, they won them by recognizing that each victory was merely a down payment on something more important. "We're not going to sit here and have a parade and celebrate because we won five games," said Belichick, after his squad had ended its tropical hex at Miami. "We just haven't done anything yet."

SALUTE
The Patriots and their fans were quite at home in the elements at Gillette going unbeaten in the regular season and winning both playoff games.

BILLS

31-0

ORCHARD PARK,
NEW YORK

SEPTEMBER 7
2003

72 DEGREES
SUNNY

Haunted by an old friend

by NICK CAFARDO

IT WAS AS IF THE BILLS WERE THE PATRIOTS AND the Patriots were the Bills. It was as if Tom Brady was Drew Bledsoe, and vice versa. It was Buffalo coach Gregg Williams being asked whether he had gotten into Brady's head, with nobody wondering if the Patriots' Bill Belichick got into Bledsoe's head, as is often the case.

After 2002's two lopsided Patriots wins, one might have expected a downtrodden Buffalo team and an upbeat New England squad, and a Patriots victory. What happened, a 31-0 Buffalo win, the worst opening day loss in Patriots history, was just the opposite.

Five days after Lawyer Milloy's release from the Patriots over a contract dispute, he was still on the winning side of a game the Bills could not have orchestrated any better. Milloy, who started at strong safety, made five tackles and was credited with an 11-yard sack of Brady. He made a key play by defending a pass in the back of the end zone intended for David Patten, enabling Nate Clements to grab the deflection for an interception.

The last starter introduced, Milloy came out with a new dance that he had especially designed for his new fans. "I don't think the Bills needed Lawyer to get them going," said Patriots guard Mike Compton. "The rest of their guys outplayed us in every phase of the game."

The Patriots were flat from the outset.

If there was one other undeniable fact about the Bills, it was that their revamped defense seems like it may be special. At least it was on this warm day before 73,262 at Ralph Wilson Stadium. To shut out the Patriots, who were last blanked Nov. 8, 1993, 6-0, by the Jets, was over-

FIRST DOWNS	RUSHING YARDS	PASSING YARDS	TURNOVERS
NE 16 | 23 BUF	105 | 104	134 | 215	4 | 2

HELLO, AGAIN
Tom Brady gets reacquainted with—and sacked by—an old friend and former teammate, Bills safety Lawyer Milloy.

SACKS	PENALTIES	TIME OF POSSESSION	RECORD
2 | 2	12 | 10	26:10 | 33:50	0-1 | 1-0

HEAVY LOAD
Sam Adams rumbles past Tom Brady while returning an interception for a touchdown.

DREW'S TURN
Drew Bledsoe shows how it feels to open the season with a win against his former teammates from New England.

whelming evidence. Newcomers Takeo Spikes and Sam Adams were big differences on a defense that ran over the Patriots, limiting Brady to a 14-for-29 effort for 123 yards and four interceptions, clearly his worst as a Patriot.

"There was nothing good that came out of that game," said Brady. "It's the first time we've faced adversity in six weeks and we've got to rebound. From the opening kickoff to the last play of the game, it was all one-sided."

Adams sealed the game when he picked off Brady with 10:24 remaining in the second quarter. The big man rambled 37 yards down the right sideline, carrying the pigskin like Ricky Williams but doing this "40" in perhaps the slowest time in NFL history. Yet blocks by London Fletcher and Aaron Schobel kept him protected, making it 21-0.

"Our defense," said an ecstatic Bledsoe, "Jeez. They were tremendous out there."

Bledsoe, who was 17 for 28 for 230 yards, with one touchdown and one interception, wasn't bad either. When Bledsoe can play with a lead, not force balls into coverage, and use his running game, it's usually going to be a long day for the opposition. Another ex-Patriot, Sam Gash, opened up good holes as a lead blocker for Travis Henry, who ran 28 times for 86 yards.

The Patriots actually ran the ball well, gaining 105 yards on 21 carries, Kevin Faulk accounting for 62 yards, but many of the runs came when the

Bills were defending a 21-point halftime lead.

The Bills stuffed it right down the Patriots' throats on their first possession, marching 80 yards in nine plays. The Bills converted two third-down plays on the drive (they were 7 for 14 on third down in the game) and Bledsoe connected on a 24-yard pass to Bobby Shaw over Ty Law and Antwan Harris. Law became animated after the play, but denied he was yelling at Harris. Said Harris afterward: "We play a team defense. If they make a play on us, it's a team mistake, not an individual one."

From the Patriots' 20, Law was called for pass interference on Eric Moulds, who had a step on him in the end zone when Law brushed his backside. On first down from the 1, Henry, behind Gash, knocked it in for the 7-0 lead.

With the temperature 72 degrees, Bledsoe kept the Patriots' defense on the field for 15 plays and 9:28 on a 90-yard scoring drive in which nothing went right for the Patriots. Third tight end Fred Baxter committed a defensive holding penalty on a punt, which would have ended the drive at the Patriots' 40. Instead, the Bills kept on moving, and Bledsoe hit wide-open tight end Dave Moore from 7 yards out for 6 more points.

After Adams's play, the Patriots went into the locker room with that huge 21-0 deficit. They have come back from such deficits before, but when they had opportunities to score they didn't take advantage.

☆ ★ ☆ ☆ ☆ ☆ ☆ ☆ ☆ ☆ ☆ ☆ ☆ ☆

EAGLES

PHILADELPHIA

31-10

SEPTEMBER 14
2003

82 DEGREES
MOSTLY CLOUDY

A turnaround for Brady

by RON BORGES

AFTER A LONG SEVEN DAYS OF POSTMORTEMS following the worst passing performance of his career in a season-opening 31-0 loss to the Buffalo branch of the Patriots, Tom Brady came back at Lincoln Financial Field as if it was still 2001. He was accurate, not antsy. He was productive, not passive. He was patient, not petulent. He was, in other words, Tom Brady, and the result was not only a 31-10 victory over the Philadelphia Eagles, but an afternoon in which he finished 30 for 44 for 255 passing yards and three touchdowns. His quarterback rating was 105.8, his highest since the Kansas City game in 2002 in which he passed for 410 yards and four touchdowns.

The difference between those two games a year apart was that last season Brady was still The Golden Boy with the Super Bowl MVP under his arm. After last week's terrible defeat, in which he threw four interceptions and finished with an abysmal 22.5 quarterback rating, that award and a lot of other things about his game had been forgotten. Suddenly there were more questions than answers about Brady and the offense he ran and Charlie Weis designed, because it had struggled in the final month last season and seemed to be beginning a new year still on its knees.

Then Brady and Co. arrived in Philadelphia and all was suddenly right with the world again. At least for the moment.

"I didn't sleep much this week," Brady said. "As a quarterback a lot of times you take pride in winning football games. When the team doesn't win and you get defeated, 31-0, and you throw four interceptions, and you get shut out for the first time in how many years, that's tough. At the same time, you need confidence to believe in yourself."

Brady got some of that confidence back in a hurry when he capitalized on two Eagles turnovers in the second quarter and turned them into back-to-back touchdown passes off play-action fakes. Both times those fakes froze the defense for just long enough to allow tight end Christian Fauria to break free in the end zone. Both times Brady found him, as he had so often last season, and those throws made the score 17-7. From that point on, the Eagles were reeling.

When he threw a third score to Deion Branch, also off play-action, midway through the third quarter to make it 24-7, it left Philadelphia quarterback Donovan McNabb in the same position Brady was in a week ago. He was playing behind the eight ball, a position that most often leads to mistakes and more misery. Not to mention some sleepless nights.

"I think we had great field position [because of the forced turnovers]," Brady said. "Our defense created great field position. We scored some points early off those turnovers to take the lead. At the point we went up 17 points, they're running uphill. With your back against the wall you can't use the full gamut of your playbook."

Brady knows well about that because he just lived it. That is how quickly things can change in the NFL based on circumstances and fortunes. One week you are in a hole and cannot get out of it. Seven days later, after a lot of tossing and turning in your bed, you are pushing your opponent into a hole just as deep.

That is life in the NFL, especially for the signal-caller.

"Certainly playing with a lead we took advantage of a lot of different situations," Brady said. "The more times you can possess the ball [the better]. The defense forcing those [six] turnovers, that was huge for us."

Against the Bills, the Patriots' offense had the ball for only three plays in the first quarter and for barely 10 minutes in the first half. Brady threw those four INTs that day, and the Bills capitalized on them.

Against the Eagles it was the opposite, with New England's offense controlling the ball for the first 20 minutes of the game to the Eagles' 10.

FIRST DOWNS	RUSHING YARDS	PASSING YARDS	TURNOVERS
NE 17 | 23 PHI	62 | 99	247 | 169	0 | 6

ON TARGET
Tom Brady gets his 'A' game back and the Patriots' first win in the bank for 2003.

SACKS	PENALTIES	TIME OF POSSESSION	RECORD
7 | 2	8 | 7	36:35 | 23:25	1-1 | 0-2

HIGH ROAD
Tedy Bruschi goes over a blocker to get at Donovan McNabb as the Patriots' defense forced six turnovers and made seven sacks.

HIGH KICK Christian Fauria gets a kick out of making a touch-down catch — one of two he made after play-action fakes by the Patriots.

☆ ★ ★ ☆ ☆ ☆ ☆ ☆ ☆ ☆ ☆ ☆ ☆ ☆ ☆

JETS

FOXBOROUGH

23-16

SEPTEMBER 21 2003

71 DEGREES SUNNY

Overcoming the pain

by NICK CAFARDO

THE EFFECTS OF MOUNTING INJURIES MAY TAKE their toll down the road, but for the second straight week, the New England Patriots looked at the casts, wraps, and braces square in the eye and laughed. Rosevelt Colvin (hip) out for the season? Ted Johnson (foot) out until Week 12? Mike Compton out with a foot injury? Injuries during the game to Ted Washington (fractured left leg), David Patten (right leg), Mike Vrabel (arm injury, extent unknown), and Ty Law (right ankle sprain)?

It didn't matter.

The JVs stepped in and played just fine as the Patriots improved to 2-1 with a 23-16 win in their Gillette Stadium home opener, a game in which the Patriots turned Jets mistakes into points while the Jets failed to convert on New England's mistakes.

It was nickel back Asante Samuel's 55-yard interception return for a touchdown to open the fourth quarter that ultimately did in the Jets (0-3). Vinny Testaverde, 39, made a terrible mistake and underthrew to Wayne Chrebet, who slipped on his break, allowing Samuel to make the biggest play of his short NFL career, juggling the ball for a moment before running to paydirt.

"Coach made a good call and put me in the right position to make the play," said the rookie corner from Central Florida. "It was a good feeling. It made me feel like I was on Cloud Nine. I was man-to-man on Chrebet and he was shifting and shaking and I waited for him to make his break. I'd never returned one for a touchdown before. Every time I'd get to the 40 and the 30 and the 20, I'd say to myself, 'You're getting closer, keep going.'"

Oh, he kept going all right, leaving Testaverde, Chrebet, and coach Herm Edwards with a sinking feeling. And yet, the Jets came back and pulled within a touchdown when a breakdown occurred in the New England secondary and Testaverde marched the Jets right down the Patriots' throats, culminating in a 29-yard strike to Chrebet with 12:53 remaining.

But that emptied the Jets' tank.

FIRST DOWNS	RUSHING YARDS	PASSING YARDS	TURNOVERS
NE 19 | 16 NYJ	147 | 65	147 | 264	1 | 1

HELPING HANDS
Deion Branch lends a
hand in the Patriots
victory with a pair of
receptions.

SACKS	PENALTIES	TIME OF POSSESSION	RECORD
0 5	9 6	32:37 27:23	2-1 0-3

It was 9-9 (three field goals each by Adam Vinatieri and Doug Brien) when the Patriots marched it 73 yards in seven plays, highlighted by a wide open 28-yard gain on a Tom Brady-to-Christian Fauria connection. On a second-and-10 from the 20, Brady threw toward Troy Brown in the end zone, and he drew an interference call on Ray Mickens, who was subbing for the injured Donnie Abraham. Mickens seemed to have great position, but he failed to turn to the ball. The ball was spotted at the 1, from where Brady, unable to find anyone open, skirted a pass rush and ran it in.

"I looked at my first read and he got caught up," Brady said. "The second guy was on the corner; he got caught up. And I looked back to Christian and he had a double team, so I kind of pumped and then fell into the end zone, it looked like. It wasn't a graceful run."

Style points aside, it was a big drive and a big play. It was the first touchdown of a game that had featured a baseball score. It wasn't entirely out of the realm of possibility that it would end as a low-scoring affair. The Patriots made a concerted effort to run the ball, control the clock, and keep their defense fresh on a warm afternoon when the game-time temperature was 71.

Rushing for 147 yards, led by Kevin Faulk (79) and Antowain Smith (55), the Patriots held nearly a five-minute advantage in time of possession. The Patriots ran 36 times and threw it only 25 times, Brady going 15 for 25 for 181 yards with no touchdowns and five sacks.

The Patriots used a makeshift offensive line, moving Damien Woody to Compton's right guard spot, and switching Joe Andruzzi from right guard to left guard. Matt Light once again did a nice job neutralizing John Abraham, who injured his hamstring later in the game and failed to get a sack.

The Patriots defense, decimated by injuries to Washington (who left the game after the fifth play and was replaced by Rick Lyle), Law, and Vrabel, made good on its promise to pay extra attention to Curtis Martin, who gained 53 yards on 15 carries. The Jets were only able to convert 1 of 13 third downs and were 0 for 2 on fourth down attempts.

The Jets had two opportunities to intercept passes and change the momentum. On the Patriots' only touchdown drive, safety Sam Garnes had the ball thrown to him at the goal line, and while he broke up the pass intended for Daniel Graham, he could have thwarted the drive.

"That's why DBs play DB and that's why they're ex-receivers," said Edwards, who also referred to a pass that slipped between linebacker Sam Cowart's hands in the late stages. Cowart could have given the Jets the ball in Patriots territory. "You can't get those back. That's what I told the guys after the game: You've got to make plays when you have a chance to make plays."

OVER THE TOP Tedy Bruschi takes the high road in an attempt to get into Vinny Testaverde's face.

47

☆ ★ ★ ☆ ☆ ☆ ☆ ☆ ☆ ☆ ☆ ☆ ☆

Coming up short

by RON BORGES

REDSKINS

LANDOVER, MD

20-17

SEPTEMBER 28
2003

65 DEGREES
PARTLY CLOUDY

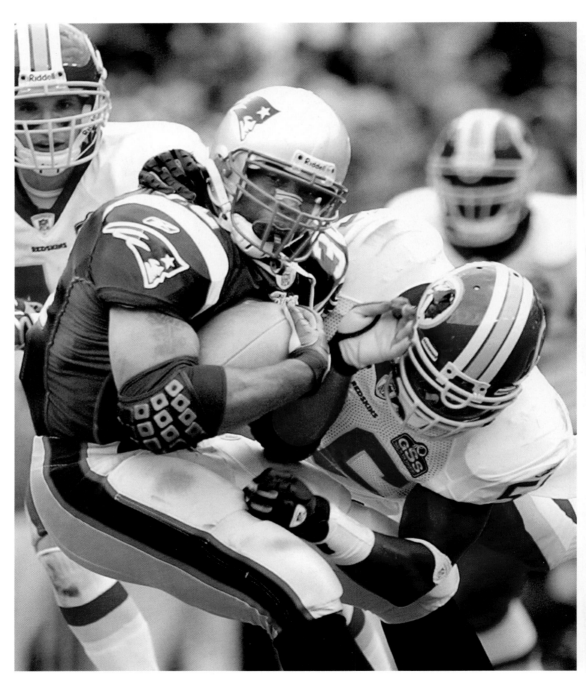

FIRST DOWNS		RUSHING YARDS	PASSING YARDS	TURNOVERS
NE 23	15 WAS	106	116	281	134	4	0

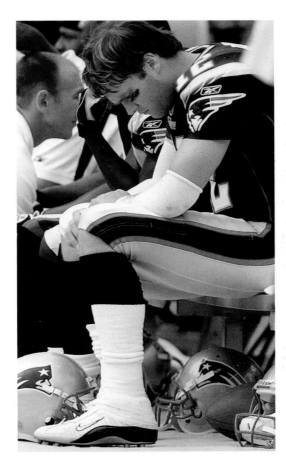

PHYSICALLY, THERE AREN'T MANY THINGS YOU would say Tom Brady does better than the other 31 starting quarterbacks in the NFL. Many of them have stronger arms. Some are more accurate passers. All but a few are more nimble. And there may be a couple—Brett Favre and Steve McNair come to mind—who are as effective a leader.

But none is a more intense competitor. In fact, there may not be a player at any position who takes losing harder than the Patriots' young QB (though if he isn't careful, he'll grow old sooner than he'd like).

That's why Brady needed a few extra moments to collect himself before leaving his locker for the interview room, where he would attempt to explain his throwing three interceptions and, for the first time in memory, failing to deliver in the clutch, leaving New England on the losing end of a 20-17 game against the Washington Redskins. Know this much: Those folding chairs in the visiting locker room at FedEx Field are pretty sturdy; they must be to have supported Brady plus the weight of the world he seemed to be carrying on his slender shoulders long enough for him to memorize the inside of his temporary quarters.

For the first two weeks of the season we've seen Brady shrug off persistent pain in his throwing elbow, but, judging by the look on his face and the way his voice quivered, it took every ounce of his pride to keep from shedding tears following a narrow defeat in which the Patriots faced fourth and 3 from Washington's 38 with 43 seconds to go.

"Everyone's real disappointed," Brady said. "More disappointment than we've had in a while because this is a game we really feel we should have won."

The Patriots trailed, 20-3, when Brady directed a 68-yard drive that ended with a 7-yard touchdown pass to Larry Centers, pulling the Patriots to within 20-17 with 2 minutes 10 seconds left. The Redskins imploded (three false starts) on their next possession, and New England got the ball back at Washington's 45 with 1:39 to go, needing only a first down to get into field-goal range.

Brady threw long and incomplete to Deion Branch on first down, to Centers for 5 yards on second down, and, following Centers's 2-yard run, behind Daniel Graham deep down the middle.

Centers implied after the game that he was open near the first-down marker on New England's final play. "If you complete it, no foul, I'm not disappointed," Center said. "Sometimes you gotta know when to take that shot. I think Tom did a pretty good job for us, we just had some unfortunate things that didn't work out for us."

Brady's judgment has been his hallmark since taking over as the starter two years ago tomorrow, but on an afternoon when he tossed up an ill-advised jump ball to Branch in the end zone— "That was probably the one that [ticked] me off the most," Brady said. "I don't even know if I reached the end zone"—that Ifeanyi Ohalete intercepted, and later tried to squeeze a deep ball to David Givens past Champ Bailey (interception No. 2), one can't help but wonder whether Brady's final decision was an uncharacteristically poor one, as well.

"We had a couple of short receivers," coach

SACKS	PENALTIES	TIME OF POSSESSION	RECORD
1|2	8|9	33:39|26:21	2-2|3-1

Bill Belichick said. "It was tight there. The Quarterback probably thought he couldn't get it in. I wouldn't second-guess that one. Troy Brown was short for first-down yardage, but I don't know if it was open."

Graham was for a moment, but the pass appeared behind him, and Ohalete broke it up. "The safety made a good play," Graham said.

Brady made quite a few nice ones himself in the second half, completing 17 of 23 passes for 198 yards and 2 touchdowns, including a pretty 29-yard TD in the third quarter that made it a game again (20-10). But he's known for making them when his team needs them most, and he didn't yesterday.

"A lot of times it comes down to execution," said Brady, dismissing his elbow trouble as a reason for his miscues. "What more can you ask for than what we had? . . . You get the ball with a minute 40 on the 45 and you can't get a first down. That's a pretty bad feeling.

"I'm a better player than that. I don't expect to make plays like that."

ROUGH DAY
Frustration was the operative word for both the New England offense, including Deion Branch (left photo) who couldn't prevent this interception, and the Patriots coach Bill Belichick (above).

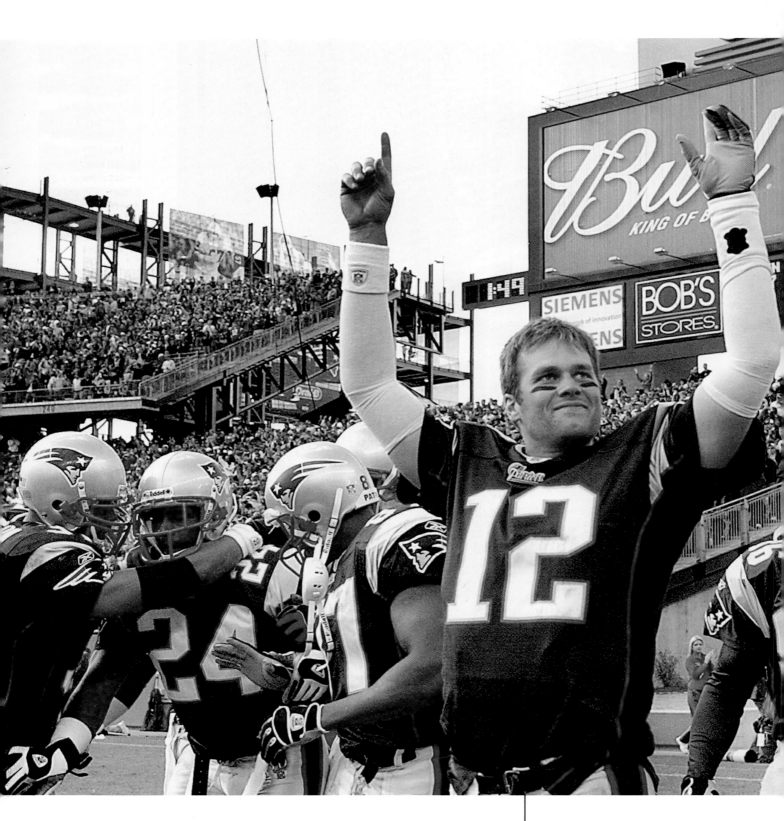

UP IN ARMS
Ty Law's touchdown got the
Gillette Stadium crowd on its
feet and the Patriots' offense,
including Tom Brady and David
Patten, fired up.

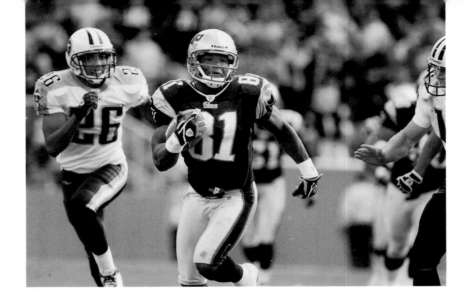

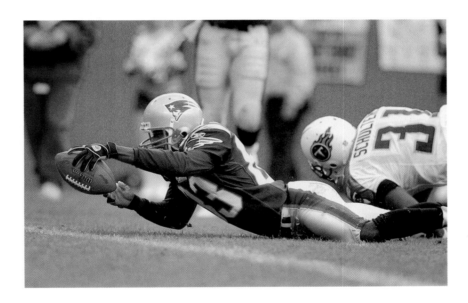

GAINING INTEREST Providing notice of the ways they benefit the Patriots were Bethel Johnson (81) with 188 return yards, Deion Branch (83) with five receptions, and Mike Cloud (21) with 73 rushing yards.

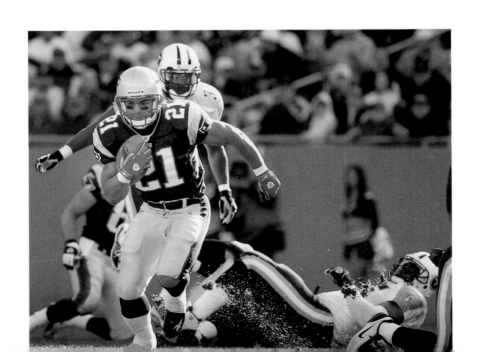

GIANTS

17-6

FOXBOROUGH

OCTOBER 12
2003

55 DEGREES
RAIN

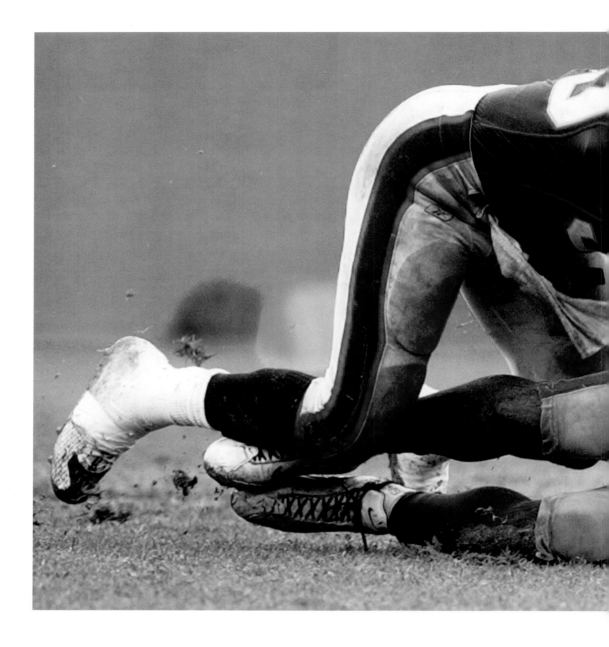

True grit

by MICHAEL SMITH

THIS WAS MORE LIKE IT. THOSE SHOOTOUTS, LIKE the one they survived with Tennessee are OK once in a while, but that isn't Patriots football. Too, you know, pretty.

Their brand of ball is gritty. Grimy. Not attractive. Just effective. When they aren't a pleasure to watch, as the Giants learned on a muddy, rainy afternoon at Gillette Stadium, the Patriots can be a pain to play. New England won, 17-6. Had the score been 170-6, it still would have been anatomically impos-

FIRST DOWNS	RUSHING YARDS	PASSING YARDS	TURNOVERS
NE 12	26 NYG	129	75	91	306	0	5

sible for Bill Belichick to wear a wider grin.

"Man, that was a great win for our football team," the Patriots coach said.

The Patriots didn't play great football. Offensively they didn't even play good football. But they played Patriots football. And that was good enough.

The defense forced five turnovers, including four Kerry Collins interceptions (two by Rodney Harrison) and a Tiki Barber fumble (forced by Tyrone Poole) that Matt Chatham returned 38 yards for a touchdown on the Giants' third play from scrimmage. The Giants had the ball for more than 10 more minutes, but the Patriots turned them away twice inside the 20-yard line and five other times inside New England's 30.

The Patriots converted just one of 11 third downs. But that one was a big one—a 21-yard completion from Tom Brady to David Givens on third-and-16 from the Patriots' 9 that kept alive

SACKS	PENALTIES	TIME OF POSSESSION	RECORD
2 | 2	10 | 8	24:47 | 35:13	4-2 | 2-3

their only touchdown drive. They had another solid game on the ground, gaining 129 yards on 31 attempts (4.2-yard average).

So no, it won't go down as one of the season's more memorable games, but this one fits in the only place that will matter come winter: the win column.

"It was just a grind-it-out type game," guard Damien Woody said. "We're not the type of team that puts up 30 or 40 points every week. We're the type of team that grinds it out. We play good, solid defense and complementary offense. A lot of our wins are going to look like this."

"Right now we're just willing ourselves," Poole said.

The Patriots were killing themselves in the first half. They went three and out on five straight possessions and moved the ball 29 yards in 21 plays. Brady went 1 for 10. They managed one first down and committed six penalties. "That was not what we were looking for," Brady said.

Still they led, 7-3, at the break thanks to three New York turnovers and two missed field goals by Brett Conway. They would have had more had they capitalized on Poole's interception of a Collins pass that was deflected by Richard Seymour on the first play from scrimmage. Adam Vinatieri missed a 42-yard field goal. (His fourth miss in his last six attempts. Worried yet?) "The defense was fantastic," receiver Troy Brown said. "They kept us around until we had a chance to get something going."

The Patriots finally got going because at halftime, out went the game plan. Offensive coordinator Charlie Weis discarded the plan designed to exploit New York's aggressiveness the way Miami had a week earlier in favor of the basics: counters and draws out of three-receiver sets against the Giants' nickel package, and short, safe passes.

The Patriots put together two scoring drives in the third quarter, a nine-play, 63-yard journey that ended with Adam Vinatieri's 28-yard field goal and a 10-play, 85-yard march to Cloud's 1-yard touchdown run. Kevin Faulk stepped in for Cloud and rushed for 85 yards on 13 carries in the second half.

"We tried to block better and eliminate plays," Belichick explained. "Charlie told the team, 'We're not going to run any new plays. Some of the runs we were going to run in this game we're going to forget about it. We're just going to run the stuff that we know and let's stop screwing up.'"

Belichick's bunch is in a position few could have imagined after a bumpy start. They've been steady in some areas, spectacular in none. In other words, they've played Patriots football.

☆ ★ ★ ☆ ★ ★ ★ ☆ ☆ ☆ ☆ ☆ ☆ ☆ ☆

DOLPHINS

MIAMI

19-13

OCTOBER 19 2003

84 DEGREES SUNNY

Swoon over Miami

by MICHAEL SMITH

SOONER OR LATER, THE HEX, THE CURSE, OR whatever it was had to end.

The streak had to end. And, unfortunately, a quality football game had to end. What a way to end them all.

Tom Brady threw an 82-yard touchdown pass to Troy Brown 9 minutes and 15 seconds into overtime at Pro Player Stadium to give the Patriots a thrilling 19-13 win—New England's first in 14 visits to Miami in September or October—only after Richard Seymour blocked Olindo Mare's attempt at a go-ahead field goal with two minutes remaining in regulation, Mare (the second-most-accurate kicker in league history) missed a 35-yarder in overtime wide right, Brady recovered his own fumble at New England's 40, and Tyrone Poole intercepted Jay Fiedler on Miami's second possession of the extra session.

"It was almost like they were trying to give it to us," Brown said. "It was a matter of time before we took advantage of it."

Guess it was just time. Thirty-seven years was enough. Sixty-nine minutes was enough. The Patriots definitely had had enough of being punked in Miami.

"It was good to get that monkey off our back, coming down here to Miami and losing for I don't know how many years in a row [five]," Brown said after his walk-off touchdown vaulted New England into first place in the AFC East by a half-game over the Dolphins. "It feels good just to come down here and get a win. It was one of those things hanging over our heads. We've been in a couple of those situations. The Jet thing, coming to New England and beating us up for four or five years [five, actually]. Coming down here and losing for I don't know how

FIRST DOWNS	RUSHING YARDS	PASSING YARDS	TURNOVERS
NE 16 | 20 MIA	59 | 97	273 | 229	2 | 3

FINISHING TOUCH
Troy Brown is on his way to scoring the game-winning touchdown in overtime.

many years in a row in September. Another one of those things to get off your back. Hopefully, next year you guys won't hang it over our heads."

Can't. They've got another streak going. The Patriots have beaten the Dolphins in overtime the last two times they've met. New England overcame a 24-13 deficit with five minutes left in last season's finale to win, 27-24, and keep the Dolphins out of the playoffs. As they did last December, the Dolphins had several opportunities to put the Patriots away. They didn't. Or, worse for their annually failed Super Bowl aspirations, they couldn't.

Miami's Jason Taylor beat Matt Light inside, but Damien Woody was there to back Light up. Brady, having play-faked and pump-faked right, drifted left and—sore elbow, sore shoulder, and all—heaved a deep pass to Brown, whose post route across the field split Dolphin safeties Sammy Knight and Brock Marion. Miami was in a two-deep zone. The Dolphins let Brown get too deep and he ended up scoring.

"Brady, I don't know how long he held onto the ball," Dolphins coach Dave Wannstedt said, "but he throws it on time, [Brown's] not going to get behind [the coverage]."

Brown, running out of "bunch" formations designed to prevent Miami's defenders from matching up with and pressing receivers, had 131 yards on six receptions. His touchdown was the longest reception of his 11-year career.

"Tom said, 'This is your play.' So I ran as hard as I could," Brown said. "I was tired of being out there. It was getting hot. Guys on defense were starting to cramp up. I wanted to finish it right there."

The Patriots looked done when Miami converted four third downs on a 16-play drive to what was assumed would be Mare's go-ahead field goal. But "Block Right Push" saved the day. They looked done again when Fiedler and Derrius Thompson hooked up on a questionable 31-yard completion on the second play of OT, and when Ricky Williams scooted for 10 and 13 yards on the next two plays to put Miami at New England's 20. But Mare was wide right.

It turned out they were never out. Most important, not at halftime (10-6, Miami), the way they were last year (16-0). "We knew coming in if we just fought them for 60 minutes—actually, today was 60-plus—we could pull it out," Woody said. "We just kept slugging it out and eventually came out winners."

SACKS	PENALTIES	TIME OF POSSESSION	RECORD
1 | 1	5 | 4	34:45 | 34:30	5-2 | 4-2

LOSING VIEWS
Olindo Mare (above) failed to convert with his chances to win the game then watched as the Patriots' offense and defense finished off Jay Fiedler & Co.

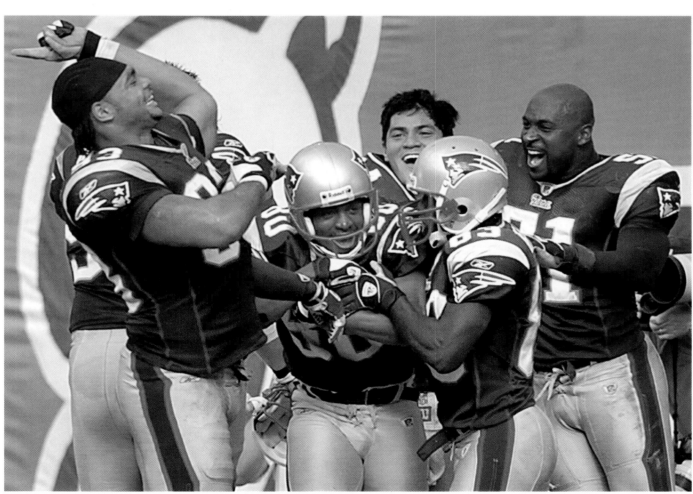

BROWNS

9-3

FOXBOROUGH

OCTOBER 26
2003

62 DEGREES
DRIZZLE

Brown
baggers

by MICHAEL SMITH

HALFWAY THROUGH THE REGULAR SEASON, the time had come for the bruised and battered Patriots to finally catch a break.

They got it in the form of a Cleveland team whose preferred quarterback, Kelly Holcomb, has a broken right fibula—a bleeding broken right fibula, actually—so painful he could not start, though he was pressed into action when starter Tim Couch sprained his right thumb near the end of the first half. A team without its stud running back, former Boston College star William Green, who sat with an injured right shoulder. A team without three of its opening-day starters on the offensive line. "Join the club, buddy," Tedy Bruschi said. "It's not a matter of who's down but who's in there and are they getting the job done."

That, in a nutshell, is the story of New England's season, one that at the midpoint has them 6-2 for the fifth time in franchise history and leading the AFC East. Getting the job done in the 9-3 win was Kevin Faulk, who contributed 154 yards from scrimmage, a career-high 96 rushing. Putting in work was second-year tight end Daniel Graham with seven catches for 110 yards, easily the best game of his career. Owed time and a half is a New England defense that allowed Cleveland to reach midfield twice and has allowed one touchdown in its last three games. Earning his check was Mike Vrabel with a career-high three sacks and a forced fumble against the team he grew up supporting. Em-

EYES WIDE SHUT
Soggy weather didn't keep the Patriots for opening holes for a career-best rushing day by Kevin Faulk.

FIRST DOWNS	RUSHING YARDS	PASSING YARDS	TURNOVERS
NE 19 | 13 CLE	94 | 84	253 | 119	0 | 1

SACKS	PENALTIES	TIME OF POSSESSION	RECORD
4|1	5|3	33:09|26:51	6-2|3-5

HOME STRETCH Mike Vrabel reaches out to Tim Couch during an impressive day by the Patriots' Ohio-born defender.

ployee of the day: Special teams coach Brad Seely, whose unit accounted for all the Patriots' points and downed four Ken Walter punts inside the 20.

There are some concerns on this week's evaluation, namely the offense's struggles in the red zone (0 for 3) and on third down (4 for 14). But the crew won its fourth in a row and sixth in seven. Boss Belichick is pleased.

"That was really about the way we expected that game to go," Bill Belichick said of his second win in three tries against his former team, this one not a done deal until Ty Law intercepted Holcomb with less than a minute to go. "Cleveland is a team that has been in a lot of close games. That's usually what it comes down to and that's certainly what it came down to today—last possession of the game."

"Some of these weeks we're going to need to score a lot more points than we did," acknowledged Tom Brady, who got the offense to the doorstep of the red zone (the 20) late in the fourth quarter before looking to Vinatieri to salvage 3 from 38. "We had some opportunities, but we really just didn't take advantage. At some

point, that's going to bite you in the butt."

The defense, sparked by the return of Law and Willie McGinest and a career game by Akron, Ohio, native and former Ohio State standout Vrabel, saved the Patriots' rears by forcing punts on eight of Cleveland's 10 possessions and allowing only three of 14 third downs to be converted. The Browns employed a lot of three-receiver sets yet managed only 119 passing yards. The Patriots sacked Couch once and Holcomb thrice, and made the poor guy run around on those bad legs more than he would have liked.

"We put a lot into this game," Vrabel said. "We knew how important it was and what time in the season we were at where you could start to go one way or another. We knew it was important, with the schedule we had coming up. We needed to win this football game."

"We played a tough game, a physical game and just were able to keep the edge," Matt Light said. "It's not always going to be pretty out there. Those guys get paid to play, too."

But it was New England's guys who really earned their money yesterday. So much so that Boss Belichick gave them a day off.

☆ ★ ★ ☆ ★ ★ ★ ★ ★ ☆ ★ ☆ ☆ ☆ ☆

BRONCOS

DENVER

30-26

NOVEMBER 3
2003

35 DEGREES
FOGGY

High and mighty

by MICHAEL HOLLEY

SOME OF THE BIGGEST NAMES IN NFL HISTORY have been on his side in his career. Bill Belichick has coached Lawrence Taylor, been on staff with Bill Parcells, and befriended Jim Brown. He has witnessed a miracle team—the 2001 Patriots— raise a Lombardi Trophy to the sky.

But with all that said, his current team may be his favorite.

Play a close game in Miami? Please. They'd rather win on an 82-yard pass from Tom Brady to Troy Brown. Stay competitive against the Titans and Eagles? Sure. They'll take wins, too, blitzing on most defensive plays against Donovan McNabb and unleashing Mike Cloud (7 carries, 73 yards) on the Titans.

Against the Broncos, the Patriots were facing a team that has haunted them since the late 1960s, when Belichick was a student at Annapolis High School. The Broncos have humiliated the Patriots here and in Foxborough. They have beaten them with Craig Morton at quarterback, John Elway at quarterback, and Brian Griese at quarterback. On a night when Al Michaels, John Madden, and the rest of the nation was watching, the Patriots won, 30-26.

They won even though they were doing their own rendition of "Scary Movie 3" in the first half. The Broncos held the ball for more than 21 minutes to New England's eight, the Patri-

FIRST DOWNS	RUSHING YARDS	PASSING YARDS	TURNOVERS
NE 17 | 18 DEN	69 | 114	350 | 163	2 | 1

NO STRETCH
Deion Branch collected three
passes for 107 yards, including a
66-yarder for a touchdown.

SACKS	PENALTIES	TIME OF POSSESSION	OPPONENTS RECORD
0 | 0	14 | 4	28:26 | 31:24	7-2 | 5-4

GOOD CALL
A win in Denver is enough to make Bill Belichick hug offensive coordinator Charlie Weis.

ots had three first downs to the Broncos' 14, and the home team had run twice as many offensive plays.

The halftime score? Broncos, 17-13.

"I've got an empty spot in my heart right now," Broncos quarterback Danny Kanell said when the remarkable game was over. "In my mind, I thought we were going to win."

So, too, did most of the 76,203 fans at Invesco Field at Mile High. It didn't look great for the Patriots a couple hours before the game. That's

when the team announced that dominating defensive tackle/defensive end Richard Seymour did not travel with the team because of a leg injury.

It was going to be difficult enough facing Clinton Portis—averaging more than 5 yards per carry—with Seymour. But stopping him with two rookies (Dan Klecko and Ty Warren) holding down the interior seemed a lot to ask.

Portis ran for 111 yards and scored the Broncos' first touchdown, but he was controlled most of the night. His performance was good; the Patriots had someone on their side who was great.

Remember, this team's official bumper sticker is, "We go beyond what you expect." Brady was the embodiment of that slogan, opening the New England scoring with a 66-yard pass to Deion Branch.

The play was executed in typical Patriots style. While the highlight shows will focus on Brady-to-Branch, the play came to life because of the behind-the-scenes work of Troy Brown. Brown was able to sell safety Kenoy Kennedy on a short pass. Kennedy bit so hard on Brown's route that he wound up hitting the receiver about 15 yards from the line of scrimmage.

This is why this team is on its way to being Belichick's favorite. He is a cerebral sort, and he loves to be surrounded by football intellectuals. It is why he still talks reverentially about Taylor and his ability to figure out the techniques being used against him. It is why he has so much admiration for Jim Brown, who was not only a dominant fullback but a dominant lacrosse player as well. And it is why he appreciates the little things—Brown's route running, Adam Vinatieri's efficiency, Brady's hunger to be better—in his current team.

If you focus on the warts, the Patriots had no business winning the game. They were extremely sloppy, accumulating 14 penalties. But they offset the sloppiness with 350 yards from Brady, a game-changing special teams move in the fourth quarter, and a winning touchdown catch by receiver David Givens.

Trailing, 24-23, with 2:51 remaining and at their 1, Belichick and special teams coach Brad Seely agreed that long snapper Lonie Paxton should intentionally snap the ball out of the end zone. That gave the Broncos 2 points and a 26-23 lead, but it also gave New England a free kick. Ken Walter, who had a weak 20-yard punt earlier in the game, responded with a 64-yard boomer to the Denver 15. Thirty-four seconds later, the Patriots had the ball and were on their way to the winning drive.

The night ended when Brady hit Givens for an 18-yard touchdown pass over Deltha O'Neal.

There wasn't much noise in the Rockies after Givens made his catch. Mostly, you heard the sounds of jubilant men in silver helmets. Belichick didn't toss his headset in the air as he did in Miami, but he probably felt like it. The coach likes to listen to the Beatles and the Allmans and Jon Bon Jovi. This team is going to cause him to switch up his soundtrack. When he thinks of the '03 Patriots and what they've done, he might want to slide "My Favorite Things" into his compact disc player.

CLOSING STATEMENTS Tom Brady (above) leaves the field happy to have thrown a game-winning touchdown pass to David Givens (left).

☆ ★ ★ ☆ ★ ★ ★ ★ ★ ★ ☆ ☆ ☆ ☆ ☆

COWBOYS | COWBOYS

FOXBOROUGH

12-0

NOVEMBER 16
2003

33 DEGREES
CLOUDY

Lone Star state

by MICHAEL SMITH

BEFORE THE GAME, NO MATTER HOW HARD BILL Belichick and Bill Parcells fought to escape the spotlight, it really was all about them. Do the two of you speak? Will you speak? How do you feel about Bill? And how do you feel about Bill? What did you learn from Bill? Are you still angry at Bill?

After the game, it was still all about them. Look, they hugged each other. What did he say? What did he say? What does this win mean to you, Bill? What does this loss mean to you, Bill?

In between, though, it really was all about the players. Just like the coaches said. And right now, Belichick has a better collection of them.

His Patriots improved to 8-2 for the second time in franchise history (1978) and maintained their two-game lead in the AFC East with a 12-0 victory over the Cowboys before a national television audience and 68,436 at Gillette Stadium. The shutout was New England's first since the third game of the 1996 season, when Parcells coached the Patriots and Belichick was his assistant, and the second time Dallas has been held scoreless in its last four games.

The Cowboys amassed more total yards and held a slight edge in time of possession, but they turned the ball over three times, once inside the Patriots 20. Tom Brady completed just 15 of 34 passes, but completions of 57 yards to David Givens and 46 yards to Deion Branch led to 9 points. His counterpart, Quincy Carter, threw three interceptions, including one in the third quarter to Ty Law with Dallas 19 yards away from making it a 2-point game.

And yes, they did embrace. "Bill congratulated

FIRST DOWNS		RUSHING YARDS	PASSING YARDS	TURNOVERS
NE 14	17 DAL	65 84	203 207	1 3

SACKS	PENALTIES	TIME OF POSSESSION	OPPONENTS RECORD
1|2	7|10	29:14 | 30:46	8-2|7-3

MOMENT OF THANKS
Bill Belichick and Bill Parcells meet in a brief public embrace after the game.

me on the win," Belichick said. "I told him I thought he had a good football team and I wished him well, and I do."

And as far as Belichick was concerned, thus ended the Battle of the Bills. "Coach Belichick told us to enjoy this win," said Ty Law, who had two interceptions, "but he reminded us that Houston is a tough team. They went up there to Buffalo and did something we didn't do, and that's beat those guys [12-10]."

"All the players knew this was big for him," guard Damien Woody said. "We're happy for him. It's one more step in the right direction for the organization."

"It's good to beat the teacher," said defensive coordinator Romeo Crennel, also a former Parcells employee. "We feel good about that. But our main focus is that we have to go to Houston next week."

The Cowboys offense had its share of problems. Dallas managed a mere 3 yards per carry and Carter struggled to a 38.0 quarterback rating. New England's defense did a lot less bending than usual.

"They played a lot better than we did," Parcells said. "We just didn't give ourselves a chance to win the game. I thought maybe there in the third quarter, where we had that one decent drive in there, if we could have got on the board there,

we might have made it close. As it happened all night, we just kind of self-destructed."

"We just tried to play physical, tried to get up in [Terry Glenn's] face and attack him at the line of scrimmage," Law said, applying New England's general game plan specifically to his former teammate and friend. "You don't want to let him find soft spots in the zone. Because once he gets running, it's probably going to be hard to catch him. Granted, he's probably faster than the majority of us out there; we have to stop him any way we can. The only way you can beat speed is with strength, and that's the way you hold the guy down."

"It was a shot game," said Givens, who missed most of the second half with a right leg injury. "Whoever hit the most shots would win the game, and we hit the most shots."

Brady hit one in the first quarter to Branch, who came free (thanks to a pick by Givens) across the middle for a 46-yard catch-and-run. Four plays later, Adam Vinatieri kicked a 23-yard field goal for a 3-0 lead. Vinatieri kicked a 26-yarder just after the 2-minute warning for the game's final points.

Law intercepted Carter in the end zone on the game's final play, Carter's second pick of the fourth quarter (Tyrone Poole).

Said Belichick, "We just find a way to win."

TO THE POINT
Kevin Faulk breaks free from the Dallas defense — if only for a moment.

☆ ★ ★ ☆ ★ ★ ★ ★ ★ ★ ☆ ☆ ☆ ☆

TEXANS

HOUSTON

23-20

**NOVEMBER 23
2003**

INDOORS

In the end, it's Brady

by DAN SHAUGHNESSY

TOUGH FEW DAYS FOR TOM BRADY. HIS APARTment was burglarized and he lost a television. Two of his passes were stolen by the Texans and he lost a fumble. He also got pancaked near his own end zone in overtime.

But he's Tom Brady and somewhere along the line the football gods sprinkled stardust on his shoulder pads. There's always another TV to be delivered and there's always another victory to be won after the game appears lost. When you are Tom Brady the road of landmines always leads to somewhere over the rainbow.

In yet another seemingly hopeless late-game situation yesterday, Brady overcame some uncharacteristic mistakes and led the Patriots to a 23-20 OT victory over the Houston Texans before 70,719 ten-gallon-mad-hatters at Reliant Stadium. Brady's gaudy numbers included 29 completions in 47 attempts for a whopping 368 yards and two touchdowns, but those don't really tell you much about what kind of a day this was for QB 12.

This was a game in which Brady made some old-fashioned Bledsoe-like blunders—trying to do too much when he'd have been better off eating the football. It was a game in which the Patriots annihilated the Texans in every offensive category except points. Brady gets much of the blame for the shortcomings, but he scrambled when he had to scramble, and converted third-down and fourth-down plays in the fourth quarter and OT when he had to make them, and somehow he willed his team to victory. Again. With Brady at quarterback, the Patriots are 7-0 in overtime games.

"It didn't look good there for a while," he said. "But it showed you we've got a lot of heart and perseverance."

After a day of mistakes and failure to capitalize, the Patriots trailed, 20-13, and faced a third-and-10 from their 33 with 2:26 left when Brady dropped back to pass and saw nothing. His miniature receivers were all covered and there were linemen in his face. At that moment, he did something very un-Brady like. He scrambled.

Brady is not Doug Flutie. Brady scrambling looks as natural as Bob Kraft dancing with Ty Law at City Hall Plaza. But he eluded his pursuers and gave Daniel Graham time to get open. He finally got it to Graham downfield for a game-saving 33-yard completion.

"I was running for my life," Brady said. "The first couple of guys weren't open. I had to spin back and roll to my right. I saw Daniel lose his guy and I just threw it. I didn't see the completion."

The big gain set up (five plays later) a fourth-and-1 4-yard touchdown pass to Graham with 40 seconds left that sent the game into OT. The TD required more improvisation from New England's signal-caller. He ran a bootleg to his right, but the Texans hadn't gone for the fake run to the left and it was clear Brady was going to lose his footrace for the first down. Instead of letting the game end on the play, he threw off his back foot, against the flow, and lofted it over coverage and into the suddenly dependable hands of Graham.

In OT, Brady could have lost the game again, but somehow he held on to the ball when he was blindsided by Jamie Sharper on a third-and-6 from his 13. A fumble would have meant the end of New England's six-game winning streak, but Brady held on, the Patriots punted, and they lived for another possession.

On the winning drive, Brady took the Patriots

FIRST DOWNS	RUSHING YARDS	PASSING YARDS	TURNOVERS
NE 29 | 11 HOU	128 | 89	344 | 80	3 | 2

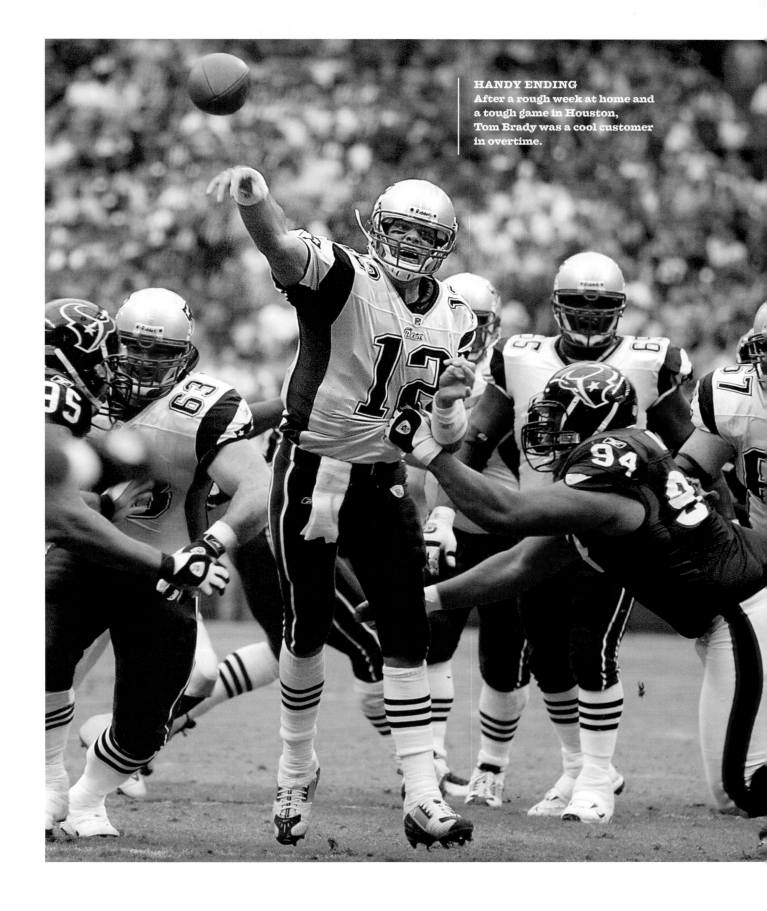

HANDY ENDING
After a rough week at home and a tough game in Houston, Tom Brady was a cool customer in overtime.

SACKS	PENALTIES	TIME OF POSSESSION	RECORD
3│4	5│6	43:50│30:29	9-2│4-7

OOPS
The unsure hands of Daniel
Graham provided clutch grabs
later against the Texans.

from their 14 down to the Houston 10, setting up Adam Vinatieri's field goal with just 41 seconds left in OT. The win gave Brady a career regular-season record (as a starter) of 29-12, which leads all active quarterbacks.

The win pushed New England to 9-2 for the first time in franchise history, but the Patriots know they won't be able to make so many mistakes (a blocked field goal and punt to go with Brady's gaffes) if they plan to return to Houston for Super Bowl XXXVIII Feb. 1.

"Tom tried to make a play and sometimes you just get hit," said coach Bill Belichick. "I'm sure Tom would like it back. But a game like his comes down to big plays, and whoever makes them deserves to win. Tom has always been great at the end of games. He's a good decision-maker. He really did a good job."

By Brady's lofty standards, it was not a particularly good job, despite the hefty numbers. A team doesn't usually win when its QB turns it over three times.

But this is 2003. This is Tom Brady. The Patriots always win. Next time they play here they'll be representing the AFC, maybe dressing in the home team's locker room.

SECOND CHANCE
Adam Vinatieri had one field goal blocked but he was on target when it counted in overtime.

79

☆ ★ ★ ☆ ★ ★ ★ ★ ★ ★ ★ ★ ☆ ☆ ☆

COLTS

INDIANAPOLIS

38-34

NOVEMBER 30
2003

INDOORS

Magic
carpet ride

by MICHAEL HOLLEY

IT'S GOING TO BE CAPTURED IN PICTURES AND songs. It's going to be the centerpiece of the Patriots' 2003 highlight video. It's going to have its own sponsorship deal. It just may be stolen in the middle of the night and passed around like a Stanley Cup.

Is it really possible for a single yard—36 inches of RCA Dome carpet—to be famous?

At the end of their draining afternoon against the Indianapolis Colts, the Patriots learned a lot about themselves. They realized that they are vulnerable enough to be shoved to the ledge. But if you're going to knock them off it, you'll need to use two forceful hands and prevent them from so much as a sliver on which to hang.

And 36 inches is far too much space.

The Patriots were able to win their 10th game of the season, 38-34, because they refused to give Edgerrin James a hole to run through. With 40 seconds remaining and the Colts with a first down at the Patriots' 2, James ran for a yard.

He tried to run up the middle on second down, and he was stopped for no gain. On third down, Peyton Manning tried to pass his way into the end zone and couldn't find rookie receiver Aaron Moorehead. On fourth down, with just 14 seconds left, the home team found itself in a strange land.

The Colts were going to be running, but they were in a passing formation. They had three receivers on the field, and the Patriots were in man-to-man coverage. Someone, either a line-

FIRST DOWNS	RUSHING YARDS	PASSING YARDS	TURNOVERS
NE 21 | 26 IND	56 | 98	226 | 272	3 | 2

SHOW STOPPERS
Eugene Wilson (26) and Willie McGinest (55) helped the Patriots to clamp down on a final rush by the high-scoring Indy offense.

SACKS	PENALTIES	TIME OF POSSESSION	RECORD
2 | 2	6 | 4	27:59 | 32:01	10-2 | 9-3

backer or a safety, was going to be unblocked.

That someone turned out to be outside linebacker Willie McGinest, who dropped James for a 1-yard loss. The game was over, and the Patriots were out of town with their eighth consecutive win.

One yard is the obvious difference between winning and losing, but it represents other things as well. It is the difference between sleeping at home and sleeping in a place where you have to dial 9 for an outside line. It's the difference between Gillette Stadium and the RCA Dome in January. It's the difference between Quincy Market and Market Square, the Mass. Pike and the Indiana Toll Road.

The Patriots now own "quality" wins over the Titans, Colts, Eagles, Cowboys, and Dolphins. Those teams are a combined 43-16. The Patriots are a playoff team that has beaten playoff teams. Their hyper defense of that 1-yard green space helps them get a little closer to playing a postseason game—or games—at home.

It's becoming more difficult to look elsewhere for the best team in the AFC. Since the Patriots have a few glaring blemishes, it can't be them, right? They have a modern-day Tony Nathan

(Kevin Faulk) as their most productive runner, Mike Cloud leads them in touchdowns with five, and Antowain Smith, one of the quiet heroes of Super Bowl XXXVI, was deactivated for yesterday's game.

When they needed to run out the clock with a late lead, the Patriots couldn't do it. Faulk fumbled with 3:53 left to set up a field goal that made it 38-34. On the next series, the Patriots burned just 20 seconds because they were forced to throw when they wanted to run.

And we haven't even talked about the struggles of punter Ken Walter.

But as Belichick said when asked about Walter yesterday, "What's out there?" What team is out there that should frighten New England?

If you mention playoffs to the head coach and his players, they'll all deflect the compliment and try to reroute the conversation. They don't spend a lot of time, publicly, dwelling on where they now stand. No one could have imagined that in September, when we were talking about one big cut— of Lawyer Milloy—instead of one big yard.

There is no doubt that the Patriots are enthusiastic this morning. They tend to put on tragedy masks to keep themselves humble, but everyone who is paying attention can see the smiles.

Yeah, they blew a 21-point lead. Yeah, Tom Brady seemed to lose his touch in the second half after completing 20 of his first 23 passes. Yeah, Manning had them retreating until the final minute.

The Patriots, though, are a proud group. Everyone who spoke yesterday talked of toughness and resolve. They know they would never allow themselves to make the excuses the Colts did following their remake of "The Longest Yard." The Colts said they couldn't get into their goal-line offense because they didn't have their regular personnel.

No, the New Englanders would have come up with something. That's what they've been doing all year.

Before Belichick left the dome, he was asked about the plane ride home. He laughed. He allowed a peek into his thoughts, saying the mood was so light that "we don't need a plane to get back."

HAPPY RETURNS, 2 Bethel Johnson gets free for another long kickoff return against the Colts.

DOLPHINS

12-0

FOXBOROUGH

DECEMBER 7
2003

28 DEGREES
SNOW

Snowballin' into the playoffs

by MICHAEL SMITH

SUCCESS WON'T CHANGE THE PATRIOTS. BETTER yet, success in December won't change the Patriots. "We've got big plans," said rookie safety Eugene Wilson. "[This is] the first step."

New England secured its second AFC East title in three seasons with a 12-0 win over the Miami Dolphins at a giant snow globe commonly known as Gillette Stadium.

If the players celebrated over any of this, they kept it brief and conducted it before outsiders were allowed into their locker room. They left the fun to the 45,378 fans, who following Tedy Bruschi's fourth-quarter touchdown used the snow that caused major logistical problems for party favors, tossing it skyward in unison. Honestly, the only visible proof that the players had accomplished anything was their commemorative T-shirts.

Blame it on Bill Belichick. The coach's tunnel-vision approach has seen the Patriots through 11 victories in 12 games and nine consecutive wins, so who are we to suggest correction? In the postgame locker room, he congratulated his team, told it to savor its first season sweep of Miami since 1997.

"Everything trickles down from Coach Belichick," said Antowain Smith, who went from the inactive list to carrying 27 times. "He's not going to let us get too high. The main thing he told us was to be humble, that it's a great victory for us, and not to take anything away from ourselves. But the job is not complete yet."

"He keeps putting goals up there for you," offensive lineman Damien Woody said. "You nev-

FIRST DOWNS	RUSHING YARDS	PASSING YARDS	TURNOVERS
NE 13 | 7 MIA	78 | 68	150 | 66	1 | 3

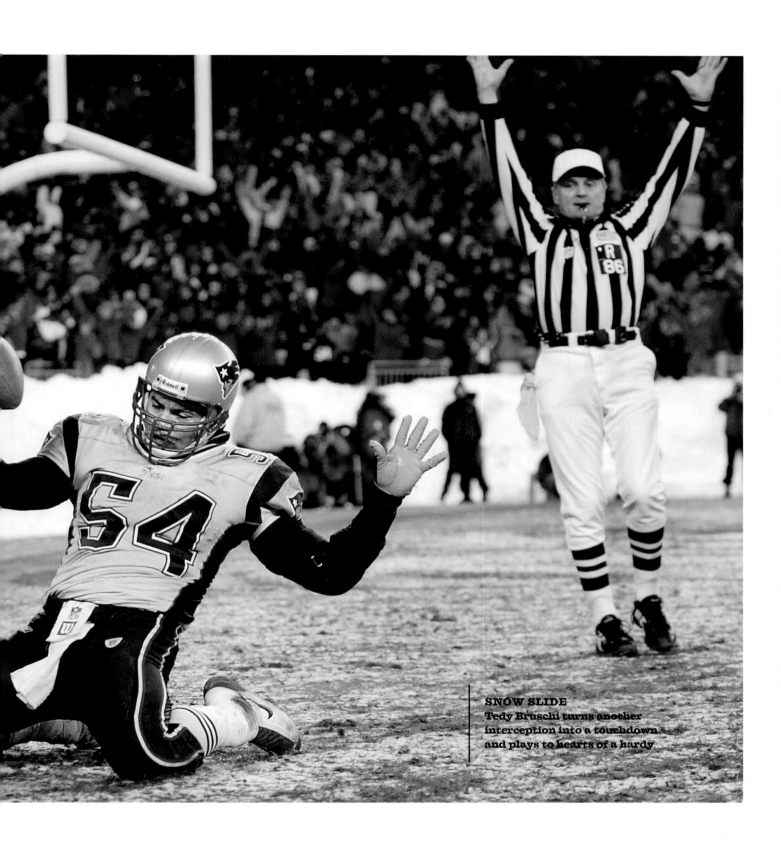

SNOW SLIDE
Tedy Bruschi turns another
interception into a touchdown
and plays to hearts of a hardy

SACKS	PENALTIES	TIME OF POSSESSION	RECORD
5|3	2|4	32:45|27:15	11-2|8-5

er want to stay the same. You want to keep going up. He always puts goals in front of us. Even after a victory like this, the goal now is to maintain the No. 1 seed and beat a Jacksonville squad that's on the rise."

Belichick did not entertain any discussion before the game about the possibility that his team would clinch a division title sooner than any other in franchise history. After it was done, he had little to say about it.

"It's one of your goals at the beginning of the year," said Belichick, whose team is tied with the 2001 edition for the most regular-season wins in Patriots history. "We're happy about it, obviously, but there's still a lot of football left to be played this year. We'll just keep looking ahead. I saw Jacksonville had a really big win and I watched a little bit of them on tape week. They're pretty good, especially defensively. This will be a good challenge for us. We have to put this one behind us and move ahead. We'll enjoy it for a couple of hours."

It was not any enjoyable three hours for Miami, the fifth opponent New England has held to 10 points or fewer this season and the second straight visitor to Gillette Stadium not to score. (Tennessee's Steve McNair, four home games and two months ago, was the last person to score a touchdown here.) If you don't think this season is special, consider that the Patriots, coming into the season, had not shut out an opponent since 1996.

The Patriots held Miami's offense to 134 yards and an average of 2.2 yards per play. They sacked Jay Fiedler five times and forced him into 13-for-31 passing, with two interceptions. Ricky Williams gained 68 yards on 25 carries. They forced a Dolphins-record 11 punts by Matt Turk.

New England's offense didn't do much, either. Tom Brady and Co. did what they had to, and that was plenty. They held the ball for 32 minutes, 45 seconds. "I certainly didn't think we racked up many statistics," said Brady (16 of 31, 163 yards, 6 completions each to Deion Branch and Daniel Graham). "There weren't many mistakes, and I think a lot of times we play to the score, and we were winning."

The offense produced Adam Vinatieri's 29-yard field goal 13:14 into the first period. The defense did the rest—Bruschi's 5-yard interception return for a touchdown with about 9 minutes remaining, and Jarvis Green's sack of Fiedler for safety with 1:13 left.

Bruschi has returned his last four interceptions for touchdowns. "It was defense where we had all the guys covered up. I peeked at Jay's eyes and there was the ball right there. I had to reach up and grab it."

And the fans proceeded to grab and toss what was left of the estimated 30 inches of snow Foxborough received over the weekend. "That was incredible, wasn't it?" Bruschi said. "Throwing the snow up in the air with the music. It got me into the holiday spirit."

☆ ★ ★ ☆ ★ ★ ★ ★ ★ ★ ★ ★ ★ ☆ ☆

JAGUARS

27-13

FOXBOROUGH

DECEMBER 14
2003

25 DEGREES
SNOW

Some of everything

by MICHAEL HOLLEY

TWELVE AND TWO IS NICE, BUT IT DOESN'T BEGIN to tell their story. The Patriots aren't just a team sitting atop a division, conference, and league. They really are a group that's big enough and diverse enough to represent an entire six-state region.

This is the team for accountants, mathematicians, and all those who see beauty in numbers. This is the team for dreamers. This is the team for streakers (no, not that kind). This is the team for serious thinkers, motivators, practical jokers, and even gifted students who sometimes lose their focus.

All of this—and a bunch of snow—was on display again at Gillette Stadium. Jacksonville was in town, and the Jaguars' logo became the latest symbolic brick to be placed in the stadium walls. The Patriots won, 27-13, to push their winning streak to 10.

Their 10-game streak is the longest in team history. Their 12 wins are the most in team history. They have allowed 22 points in their last five home games, which is one of the best defensive runs in any team's history. They have allowed 68 points at home, and 30 of those came in one game.

At times, the Patriot coaches must feel like teachers trying to come up with a demanding curriculum. Bill Belichick and his staff are constantly challenging the players to achieve a goal that has eluded them.

Some of the targets are obvious (win the game, don't turn over the ball). Others are directed at specific game situations. One of the Patriot challenges was to score on the opening drive. After about five minutes and 66 yards, the team had wiped another item from the coaches' charts.

FIRST DOWNS	RUSHING YARDS	PASSING YARDS	TURNOVERS
NE 18	17 JAX 84	72 212	282 1	2

	FIRST DOWNS	RUSHING YARDS	PASSING YARDS	TURNOVERS
NE	18	84	212	1
JAX	17	72	282	2

GOOD HANDS
Rookie David Givens shows why his hands are becoming dependable targets for Tom Brady.

SACKS	PENALTIES	TIME OF POSSESSION	RECORD
1 | 2	4 | 8	32:41 | 27:19	12-2 | 4-10

TOO SOON
Premature celebration kept Tyrone Poole from finishing off this interception return with a touchdown dance.

But there's always something.

As much as Belichick enjoys leading a team with 12 wins, he is forever fearful of complacency and arrogance. The coach counts Jim Brown as a close friend; you would have thought he was talking about Brown when he described Jaguars running back Fred Taylor before this game. Most fans probably have noticed how much Belichick has downplayed wins lately.

Remember, this was the same man who threw his headphones in the air in Miami and was extremely complimentary of everyone in Denver. Not now. He knows there are fewer dissenting national voices when it comes to the Patriots. He knows that his players can't sing the "nobody believed in us" refrain, because it seems that everyone believes lately.

So when there is even the slightest sign of a lapse, he reacts. Rookie receiver Bethel Johnson did not have a strong week of practice, so he was inactive for yesterday's game. Belichick is intrigued by Johnson's speed and potential, but not intrigued enough to put Johnson on the field when he is drifting during practice.

The coach is a fan of Tyrone Poole, who has played like a Pro Bowler at cornerback. But Poole realizes that some coach may make an example out of him. Poole intercepted two passes. On his second pick, he had a 44-yard return and appeared to be headed for a touchdown. He held the ball up near the 5, thinking he had a clear path to the end zone.

He didn't.

He was tackled at the 3.

An interviewer asked him if the name Leon Lett sounded familiar. He smiled. Lett is the former Cowboys defensive lineman who celebrated a touchdown too early in the Super Bowl and had the ball stripped from him on the way to a score.

"I didn't fumble," Poole said. "I wasn't in the same area [with Lett]. I may be the next-door neighbor, but I'm not in the same house."

Belichick has been known to use books (Sun Tzu's "Art of War"), songs, and videos to motivate his team. He'll be at it again for the next of couple weeks. He knows what's in front of his team now: a chance to win out and, ultimately, secure the right to play in the sloppy weather of the Northeast.

This team doesn't view The Streak as a streak. It sees the game as one episode out of 16.

In the latest episode, the Patriots held Taylor to 57 quiet yards. They got touchdowns from Troy Brown and Daniel Graham. They got an efficient game from Tom Brady. They proved once again that they know what they're doing, even when they are playing in snow.

These Patriots, built by white-collar workers and sustained by blue-collar employees, truly belong to the region. Yesterday, for the 10th consecutive game, they produced an episode that was an all-ages show.

Eleventh hour

by MICHAEL SMITH

JETS

EAST RUTHERFORD,
NEW JERSEY

21-16

DECEMBER 20
2003

30 DEGREES
CLEAR

BASED ON THE HISTORY OF THIS SERIES, IF there was a game that posed the biggest threat to the Patriots' winning streak, "Jets at the Meadowlands" was the one.

The threat was real, but the streak remains intact.

The 2003 Patriots extended their franchise record with their 11th straight, a 21-16 takedown of the Jets before a national television audience and 77,835 at the Meadowlands.

It was again the Patriots defense that made the difference. The Patriots intercepted Jets quarterback Chad Pennington five times, including one that Willie McGinest returned 15 yards for a touchdown in the second quarter that gave the Patriots' a lead they would hold for the rest of the evening. Another of Pennington's picks, by Tedy Bruschi, led to New England's first touchdown. Still another, Ty Law's pick in the end zone in the third quarter, ended a Jets scoring threat. Safeties Rodney Harrison and Eugene Wilson also had interceptions.

"Getting those scores early, that was important," coach Bill Belichick said. "We were able to play most of the game from ahead, which was good."

Bruschi's leaping interception over the middle on New York's second play from scrimmage gave the Patriots possession at the Jets' 35. On the next play, Tom Brady and David Givens collaborated on a 35-yard touchdown, giving the Patriots a 7-0 lead 48 seconds into the game.

New England did not score a touchdown on its first possession in its first 13 games. The Patriots have done it two weeks in a row.

Givens would later catch his team-leading fifth touchdown of the season, a 5-yarder on the first drive of the third quarter.

The Patriots' early lead didn't last long, however. Actually, it did. About 9:20. Pennington responded by directing the Jets on a 16-play, 83-yard drive that ended with his 1-yard touchdown run. The Patriots had the play-action pass covered well on third and goal but Pennington kept rolling out until he reached the end zone.

McGinest broke the 7-7 tie with his interception return 1:26 into the second quarter. On third and 2 from his 15, Pennington tried to hit Curtis Conway on a slant. McGinest, in perfect position, used his 6-foot-5-inch frame to leap and deflect the pass. A la Asante Samuel in Game 3, McGinest caught the deflection and took it to the end zone. It was the Patriots' league-leading sixth defensive touchdown this season.

With 1:55 to go before intermission, the Jets took over at their 25. Eighty-four seconds later, they were at New England's 5, but the Jets had to settle for Doug Brien's 29-yard field goal and a 4-point deficit at halftime.

Pennington, who scored both New York touchdowns on runs of 1 and 10 yards, never had thrown more than two interceptions in any of his first 26 games (19 starts). The Jets' five turnovers equaled a third of their giveaways through their first 14 games—15, the second fewest in the league.

The previous time the Patriots faced Pennington, he picked them apart, passing for 285 yards and three touchdowns. That was last year, before Bill Belichick overhauled his secondary. In the rematch, Pennington just got picked. And picked. And picked.

"We tried to disguise a lot, move around a lot," Harrison said. "To be honest with you, you can disguise all you want against good quarterbacks, but it comes down to guys making plays."

Antowain Smith carried 18 times for a season-high 121 yards—New England's first 100-yard rusher in 22 games. Smith broke runs of 30 and 23 yards, his longest of the season.

"It's all about attitude," Damien Woody said. "That's one area they're deficient at on defense, is rush defense [31st in the league coming into the game], so that's one area you want to go after them in. Everybody across the board did a good job of getting after guys."

FIRST DOWNS	RUSHING YARDS	PASSING YARDS	TURNOVERS
NE 13 | 22 NJY	133 | 109	138 | 212	1 | 5

MAKING A POINT
Willie McGinest celebrates his touchdown after intercepting a pass—one of five by the Patriots.

SACKS	PENALTIES	TIME OF POSSESSION	RECORD
4 0	5 4	27:21 32:39	13-2 6-9

BILLS

31-0

DECEMBER 27
2003

42 DEGREES
SUNNY

A perfect finish

by NICK CAFARDO

ON A ROLL
Daniel Graham comes down with a touchdown catch during the regular-season finale.

HOME-FIELD ADVANTAGE THROUGHOUT THE playoffs. Revenge. Offensive and defensive domination. An 8-0 record at Gillette Stadium. A 14-2 regular-season record.

The closest thing to a perfect season, and the Patriots' best regular season ever, concluded at Gillette Stadium yesterday with a poetic 31-0 splattering of the Buffalo Bills. Buffalo appeared to pack it in even before the opening whistle and never challenged the Patriots, who won their 12th straight game.

The score was sweet revenge, matching the Week 1 thrashing of the Patriots by the Bills.

The Patriots' third shutout of the season was preserved by a Larry Izzo interception of Bills backup quarterback Travis Brown in the end zone with 13 seconds remaining.

"All 53 guys wanted to keep that zero on the scoreboard," said Izzo. "You have to give credit to everyone in this locker room. It wasn't just one play. It was 60 minutes of football."

There was no Gatorade splash of coach Bill Belichick late in the game. There was no large celebration in the locker room. This is a team that knows that if it doesn't win the Super Bowl, the regular season doesn't mean much.

The game showed the opposite paths former teammates Tom Brady and Drew Bledsoe are on. Bledsoe was 12 for 29 for 83 yards with one interception. Brady was 21 for 32 for 204 yards and threw four touchdowns in the first half. It was a rather sad performance by Bledsoe (34.7 rating in the game), one of the troika of personalities who saved Patriots football in the early '90s along with owner Robert Kraft and former Patriots coach Bill Parcells.

"Some people might look at the scoreboard and say Buffalo laid down. They fought hard and we whupped them," said Patriots linebacker Matt Chatham.

If that was the case on the field, it didn't look that way from afar. It looked like Bledsoe was on

FIRST DOWNS		RUSHING YARDS	PASSING YARDS	TURNOVERS
NE 26	16 BUF	131 82	190 174	1 4

an island, and the New England defense was in a feeding frenzy. It held the Bills to 256 yards and the time of possession was almost seven minutes in New England's favor.

Already trailing, 7-0, Bledsoe was hit as he threw his first pass of the game when Tedy Bruschi roared in on a blitz. Bledsoe's dying quail was picked off by Mike Vrabel and returned 14 yards to the Bills 34.

From there, the Patriots scored their second touchdown on a 9-yard pass from Brady to Bethel Johnson.

"It all happened pretty fast," said Johnson, the rookie who became one of Brady's favorite targets. "I don't know what coverage they were in, but they were pretty much leaving me out there by myself the whole time. Tom just recognized it and threw it on in."

OUT LOUD
A third home shutout was one of many things inspiring the Patriots' defense and Tedy Bruschi.

SACKS	PENALTIES	TIME OF POSSESSION	RECORD
4|2	4|10	33:08|26:52	14-2|6-10

REFLECTIONs Tedy Bruschi Jr. and Sr.

PHOTOGRAPHS